CHRIST
AND THE
HIDDENNESS
OF GOD

Don Cupitt

SCM PRESS LTD

© Don Cupitt 1985

334 01925 7

First published 1971
by Lutterworth Press
Second Edition 1985
by SCM Press Ltd
26–30 Tottenham Road, London

Printed in Great Britain by
Billing & Sons Ltd, Worcester

CONTENTS

PREFACE TO THE SECOND EDITION

"I AM a Cambridge Lati-tudi-narian", said my supervisor George Woods, in his high precise voice; and so, with qualifications, was I. A merciful Providence had bestowed upon the English people the most reasonable form of Christianity in existence; and this Church, the Church of England, had herself been at her sanest and most perfect in the century between Archbishop Tillotson and Archdeacon Paley. The two best books on the philosophy of religion had been written by David Hume and Joseph Butler. It was all plain sailing: from a background in natural science I had graduated painlessly to a moderate version of British Empiricism and to eighteenth-century moral philosophy. I gathered that philosophy had mysteriously ceased with Kant, but had fortunately been revived in Cambridge by Moore and Russell, who were both still alive. "I've waded through endless pages of Kierkegaard," continued George Woods, "but couldn't make anything of him." I was silent, for I was reluctant to confess that I had surreptitiously begun reading Kierkegaard on the side.

When a few years later the radical theology of the 1960s appeared, it did not greatly affect me—or not at first. I did indeed make the pilgrimage to the strange Lancashire wasteland where Werner and Lotte Pelz, the authors of *God is No More* (1963) had been sentenced to dwell. Werner enjoined me to get up to date by studying Blake and Nietzsche, but I did not heed this advice till long afterwards. The direct confessional style of Harry Williams and the Feuerbachian essays of John Wren-Lewis impressed me, but if they had any influence it was slow-burning and subliminal. The early non-cognitive philosophies of religion then appearing were mostly rather slight, but I see that Paul Van Buren and D. Z. Phillips do both make a mark on these pages. As for the new movements in French thought at that time, we knew nothing of them, for the Channel was wider than the Atlantic.

Thus although this book was written during the summers of 1968 and 1969, it is not in the popular sense a typical Sixties product. Rather, we find here what looks in retrospect like a sort of manifesto, a first statement of a whole series of themes, problems and perplexities which were to obsess me permanently. The puzzles have arisen as British-style logical empiricism, which takes an instinctively realist view of religious beliefs, begins to feel itself seriously challenged by various post-Kantian currents of thought which tend in an anti-realist direction. These newer traditions include existentialism, various sorts of pragmatism such as H. L. Mansel's regulative theory of religious truth, and the ideas of Wittgenstein and his followers. Those who think that I have moved too precipitately in recent years can see, in this book and in such successors to it as *The Leap of Reason* (1976) and *Jesus and the Gospel of God* (1979), that in fact I moved only very slowly over a period of a dozen years. The main difference is that in this book of 1971 my instincts remain on the side of realism, even though I do not in fact find myself able to deliver much of what the realist is asking for; whereas in 1980 I was beginning to argue in the opposite direction and say that the will-to-realism (deep-rooted in me as in everyone else) was after all a profound religious mistake.

The shift was not quite so great as it at first seems, for in *Christ and the Hiddenness of God* I had already assimilated the anti-realist point of view, and was trying to incorporate the constructive points that it makes into my account. Thus in the original Introduction I asked, "Do statements about God purport to be descriptive assertions about an actual being?", and answered:

6

Many philosophers and some theologians reply, yes, obviously. People want to know if there is a God, and if so, what he is like. Traditional theistic religion was always realistic in its language, and it is sophistry to pretend otherwise.

But many theologians and some philosophers think this reply too crude. For one thing, traditional theism always insisted on the hiddenness of God and the inadequacy of all our ideas of him. They would say that a religion is a complex way of living and speaking which you must take part in if you are to understand it. You cannot abstract the word "God" from that context, or try to justify belief in God, without serious distortion. The word "God" does not so much designate an individual as rather express in a shorthand way the structure of a certain form of life.

I agree with the first party that theology, to be true to religion, must continually strive for objectivity, but I agree also with the second that it is in principle (not just in fact) not completely attainable. That is, I try to show the restless iconoclastic character of belief in God, which continually strives after intelligible content, and yet must by its own inner dialectic always negate any proposed specific content. We think God through human imagery, and yet deny its adequacy: we must so think, and we must so deny. The clues to the interpretation of monotheism are the old polemic against idolatry, and the insolubility of the problem of analogy.

This is already very close to my present position. The main difference is that in 1971 I was still ready to align myself with that mainstream of theological writing which almost identifies orthodox faith with the will-to-realism, the quest for objectivity; whereas now I am not.

In the case of God the considerations that were leading me to question received assumptions had to do with the problem of analogy and the dynamics of the spiritual life. In the case of Christ they had to do with the Resurrection. Looking back at the innumerable modern controversies on this subject, what strikes one is the way the orthodox realist demand appears to be in principle unsatisfiable by any coherent account. In a well-known essay in the symposium *Foundations* (1913), B. H. Streeter offered a very conservative "objective-vision" theory.

He accepted the historicity of the empty tomb. Recognizing that the risen Christ was no longer mortal nor a physical object in Nature, he argued that the Christophanies had been veridical visions, genuine self-manifestations of the glorified Christ, rather as in the Old Testament God is represented as manifesting himself in human form, or the form of an angel.

This account, one might think, is as 'objective' as could be. Yet still the orthodox were dissatisfied, and attacked him fiercely. What were they asking for? Not an event like the raising of Lazarus, for the resuscitated Lazarus is still a natural, mortal human person. Not, let us hope, an event like the bringing to life of Frankenstein's monster, for that would reduce Christianity to the grossest superstition. And if a body must be involved, then what is a body which is not a natural body? The orthodox have never said exactly, and the Church has never in fact defined the Resurrection. Thus it was in this particular case of the Resurrection that I began to think that the realist demand for objectivity was confused and unsatisfiable. Nothing could meet it, and an alternative account had to be found. Already wary of placing too much reliance on a supernaturalist ontology, and warier still of grounding Christian belief on supernatural historical events, I gave an answer reminiscent of John Wisdom: coming to believe is not a matter of discovering some extra supernatural facts, but of a change in the conceptual framework under which one perceives all the facts. This change can be brought about by argument, and may be sealed by a visionary moment of revelation. The arguments that led to the Easter faith are then logically prior to the Easter appearances.

Christology along these lines—historical facts plus interpretative theological concepts—leans heavily on history. I took what might be called a historical realist view of Jesus, in the traditional liberal manner, and have only retreated from it very reluctantly. In particular I clung to his end-of-the-world apocalypticism and to what I believed to be his *ipsissima vox* in the parables and reversal-sayings, building a good deal on them in a way that made it all the harder to surrender them. One reason for this tenacity was that I thought the Jesus-in-the-Synoptic-Gospels was a surer and more public anchorage for faith than the Christ-of-present-experience, of whom from the very beginning I found it hard to take a realist view. Somehow I felt that the notion that faith is a matter of intuitive acquaintance with an invisible person, inside one's head or behind the scenes, is epistemologically and psychologically deeply wrong. No satisfactory sense can be made of it. In fact I think it has only developed since the seventeenth century and is an aberration, the chief symptom of modern Christianity's dangerous slide into irrationalism and the cult mentality. This book fires the opening shots in a struggle to check that slide and restore rationality to the spiritual life. Whether my efforts have been along the right lines or have been fundamentally misconceived is strangely enough not my concern. Others must judge, and time will tell.

D.C.

NOTE

Footnotes can spread like weeds, and I have allowed them only where the reader may positively demand them. In citing books I refer to the editions readily available in Britain. American editions may differ in date, pagination and even title. I have tried to allow for this, where necessary, by giving chapter numbers, so that a determined reader should be able to track my source.

D.C.

Part One:

THE LIMITS OF THOUGHT ABOUT GOD

OBJECTIONS TO BELIEF IN GOD

Theism and its social context

This book begins and ends with an attempt to make sense of belief in God, though between the beginning and the ending we shall follow a rather winding path. By belief in God I mean ethical monotheism (or monotheism or simply theism) : that is, belief in and commitment to one supreme being, unsurpassed and unsurpassable in reality and goodness, who is the *archē* (the ground, or principle or beginning) of all things, and is the only possible proper object of religious commitment and worship. His relation to the world and to mankind is expressed in analogies drawn from human personality and human social life which are usually held to be in some way authorized or revealed. These analogies are universally admitted to be imperfect, but are necessary to make the religious life possible. When I use the term "theism" I mean some such belief as this, a belief which is more or less common to a large number of religions. In some religions, such as Islam, theistic belief is central and constitutive. In others, such as Hinduism, it is one possible option in a complex tradition. In others, such as many forms of primitive religion, it may be latent in that one deity is the progenitor of the rest of the pantheon. Amun-Re is "Father of the fathers of the Gods". Theism has existed in many and various forms.

Immediately we see one reason why theism raises intellectual difficulties. In a modern university, where the word "cosmology" figures in the syllabus, it is likely to be studied in departments of applied mathematics or theoretical physics, rather than in departments of theology or even philosophy. If we ask what the nature of the universe ultimately is, how it came into being, and in what direction it is evolving, we look to the natural scientist rather than to the myth-maker to supply us with models or analogies. In so doing we are true to the origins of Western speculation among the presocratic philosophers. They were technologists, as well as natural philosophers, and in their speculations about the *archē* of things they drew analogies from the movement of the water-courses which supplied their cities, from evaporation and condensation, from the tension in a lyre-string, from the centrifugal force in a rotating potter's wheel, or from the numerical proportions between musical notes.[1] By technology, in Cicero's phrase, men create a kind of "Second Nature" which in turn supplies models for understanding the workings of nature. We still stand in this tradition. Human ingenuity devises digital and analog computers which in turn suggest models for understanding the workings of human intelligence. Modern cosmological speculations derive from laboratory work in nuclear and particle physics, rather than from religion.

Our civilization is built on highly-developed mathematical, analytical, experimental and technical skills. But our social and moral perceptions are less acute. In the early Middle Ages, in Western Europe, the Church at one time prohibited marriage within the seventh degree of consanguinity; which seems to mean that the prohibition extended to sixth cousins. In advanced industrial society relatively few people can name even their second cousins accurately. We are astonished at the Australian aborigine's countless initiation rites, and the Brazilian village where the layout of the houses is a visible sign of the kinship-structure of the community. Our social perceptions are not rich enough for us to be able easily to enter so complex a world.

Yet religion proposes to relate men to what is ultimate through personal and social imagery. Although the mono-

----

[1] Benjamin Farrington, *The Faith of Epicurus* (1967), Chap. 3, has a valuable discussion of this point. Cicero's phrase in *On the Nature of the Gods*, II, 60.

theism of ancient Israel is in a way very much simpler than the polytheistic cults of some neighbouring nations and empires, it still raises great difficulties for us. We simply lack confidence in the ultimacy of the personal. We feel Pascal's problem. When a man of the Middle Ages looked up into the night sky he looked into a brilliant society. When Pascal looked up he saw a vast impersonal silence, dark and dead.[1]

Yet the doubt which the religious man may feel about the power and adequacy of his imagery, its grip on reality, is not peculiar to him. It is felt throughout the humanities, for example when a man who loves poetry and knows what it has been asks himself what poetry is today. I heard lately of a research student in English who, when he is asked by people at home what his topic of research is, says hurriedly, "Physics"!

There is a climate of opinion about which suggests to us that scientists deal in hard facts, arts men in subjective opinions; that scientists in their research are original and creative workers, and arts men commentators.

So it has been argued that religions become obsolete because the intelligibility of any particular religious language depends upon a certain social context. For example, in the Middle Ages and up to the seventeenth century it was well-nigh impossible *not* to believe in God. But the long process of secularization has gradually removed the cultural context which made belief intelligible. We have come to a time when we apprehend the world, describe it, and cope with it in ways which have no connection with the concept of God.[2]

But some qualifications need to be made to this picture of religion being evacuated of meaning and at last eliminated by the progress of scientific culture. For one thing, it is far from clear that the arts are dead. We do not yet have enough

[1] C. S. Lewis, *The Discarded Image* (1964), describes the contrast in Chap. V.

[2] Alisdair MacIntyre, "Is Understanding Religion Compatible with Believing?" in *Faith and the Philosophers*, ed. John Hick (1964).

evidence to justify the claim that everything that Shakespeare says in an impressionistic and inexact way will one day be said in an orderly and exact way by the sciences of man, or even to be sure that such a claim makes sense.

In the second place theism from the beginning employed imagery derived from technology, when it spoke of God as maker or creator of the world, rather than as begetting it. Farrington suggests[1] that Anaximander's brilliant cosmological speculations owed something to seeing a potter's wheel, and steam from a boiling kettle condensing. Certainly his drum-shaped earth in stable equilibrium looks very like a lump of clay centred properly upon the wheel, and his account of the formation of the heavenly bodies reads as if he imagined a spinning mass throwing off a spiral of steam which condenses into orbiting drops.[2] But Anaximander's contemporary in Israel, Jeremiah, also went down to learn from the potter.[3] The difference is that Anaximander's attention was concentrated on the behaviour of the clay, Jeremiah's on the hands of the potter. The Israelites were interested in technology, and they did not suppose that its secrets had been stolen by men from the Gods. They did not oppose religion and technology: on the contrary, it could probably be shown that every trade and craft known to them at one time or another furnished imagery for theism—the refiner's fire, the metal worker's forge, the irrigation of dry land, bleaching with fuller's earth, building, and working clay on the wheel.

Finally, there is a subject called theology, which, if it makes any claims at all, must also make the second-order claim that its claims are not simply relative to a particular culture. It purports to say things about God which are perennially true. Theologians sometimes try to disarm critics by saying that theology is not something which is necessary in

[1] *Op. cit.*, pp. 39–40.
[2] Texts in G. S. Kirk and J. E. Raven, *The Presocratic Philosophers* (1957). See especially fragments 119, 123–126.
[3] Jeremiah 18:1ff.

its own right, but which was developed in answer to heresy. But the real question is how theological statements can be true *or* false, how theology is possible at all.

Religion and Theology

For its starting-point theology need presuppose nothing more than the fact of religious belief and utterance. For it would seem that every religious utterance, whether addressed to God or to a fellowman, implies some theological belief. A religious utterance has some such form as this: "I testify that God is p." There are two elements in it, which we may call the confessional and the theological, and what makes it a *religious* utterance is the union of the two, the way in which the speaker commits himself, in what he says, to some assertion about God. The fact that self-involving language is used is not enough by itself to make the utterance a religious one, for we use self-involving language on other occasions such as promise-making, declaring love or war, or giving evidence. On these occasions God is often invoked, by an oath, to witness the self-commitment, but he need not be. When a man commits himself to some assertion about God, he uses self-involving language to insist that he believes his assertion to be true, and is committed to defending it if its truth is impugned.

He believes his assertion to be true, but we must distinguish between a man's being reasonable in holding a belief, and the justification of that belief. It is possible to be reasonable in holding a false belief. In antiquity it was no doubt reasonable to believe that the sun sinks below the earth at night, for observation of sunsets strongly suggests as much, and most people in fact did so believe. But that belief, though reasonably held, was erroneous, for we can now bring forward a great number of considerations which suggest a different interpretation of the phenomena. Professor MacIntyre, in the paper referred to above, was presumably saying that in the Middle Ages it was reasonable to believe in God (because such a belief was integral to the prevailing world-view) whereas now it is not reasonable (because the prevailing world-view is non-theistic). Perhaps at the time when he wrote the paper he thought that a belief such as belief in God cannot be justified (or shown to be unjustified) absolutely. The most you can hope to show is that belief in God makes sense and is reasonable in one social context but not in another. There are no quite general criteria of intelligibility and reasonableness and there is no absolute frame of reference, at least where religious belief is concerned.

However, a man who looks at the earth and the sun from a spacecraft can surely say to himself that, though he understands why people once thought that the sun sinks below the earth, their belief was in fact unjustified, and the truth of the matter is that the appearance of sunset is produced by the observable relative motions of two spherical bodies in space. And a believer who makes an assertion about God surely would not accept that what he asserts is relative to a particular culture. He makes much use of words like *forever, eternal, unchanging,* and *everlasting.* And the sort of theology which derives from Plato and which some modern writers stigmatize as "objectifying" does make it its business to abstract, to systematize and to try to justify the theological beliefs which are implicit in religious utterance.

So understood theology is not an artificial or tiresome complication. Newspaper leader-writers sometimes use the word "theological" to mean foolish and hair-splitting, when describing ideological disputes within a political party. They frequently mention medieval theologians discussing how many angels could dance on the head of a pin. But those theologians never existed: the story is a renaissance *canard.* So-called "objectifying" theology was trying to do something important and apparently straightforward, namely to systematize and clarify the beliefs about God which are embedded in Christian discourse. This involved complex argumentation, and there were elaborate attempts to justify beliefs about God.

There is a widespread tendency nowadays to doubt the

usefulness of argument in theology, and even to deny it any real place. Faith is seen as a voluntary, rather than an intellectual act. The main source of this tendency is to be found in the Lutheran tradition. The older Lutheran theologians allowed that faith is at least in part an intellectual act. They distinguished three elements in the act of faith. There was *notitia* (knowledge), the mind's entertainment of a proposition as a possible object of belief; *assensus* (assent) the mind's acknowledgement of the truth of the proposition so presented; and finally the act of will, *fiducia* (trust) by which the believer appropriates to himself and makes his own the truth thus acknowledged.

But the heart of Lutheranism always was the salvation of the believer rather than the description of God: it cares for the act of will by which faith is divine and saving more than for the act of the intellect by which it is a kind of knowledge. And so they subordinated *notitia* and *assensus* to *fiducia*, the voluntary element in faith. They asserted a certain primacy, where religion is concerned, of the will over the intellect. The influence of the principal modern philosopher, Kant, has given an enormous impetus to this way of thinking, and has led to scepticism about the aims and methods of the older "objectifying" theology.

We shall consider "confessional theology" as I shall call it, in the next chapter. If we are in the end led to something like its conclusions, it will be by way of studying from within, exploring the inner dialectic, of the older sort of theology. Where I differ from the existentialist theologians is in desiring to make a plea for the propriety and indeed necessity of argument in theology. I suspect that too many theologians reason that theology of revelation was always a matter for faith *as opposed to* argument, that natural theology is now abandoned, and therefore there is now little scope for argument in theology. On the contrary, I shall maintain that even the Christological beliefs are matters of argument, and that indefensible beliefs are empty. It is itself a logical error to suppose that the only alternatives are formal demonstration and pure fideism. Between these extremes there is scope for all kinds of informal logic.

Theological statements

If now we turn to study theological statements, in the strict sense of statements about God, there is no doubt that we do run into acute difficulties. They are familiar, for they have been much discussed in recent years.[1] In repeating them here I want to make a new suggestion about the character of these difficulties.

To be able to move, a theology needs to include at least one affirmative statement about God: a statement, that is, expressing a proposition whose logical subject is God. In order to be able to make this statement it is necessary to be able to single out or identify God, its subject. He must be indicated, or designated by means of some description. And here the difficulties begin.

It may seem absurd to claim that it is not possible to refer clearly to God, for people surely do talk and argue about God a great deal. Yet everyone who has argued about God has wondered whether he and his interlocutor are arguing about the same thing, and then perhaps gone on to wonder how it could be decided whether they are talking about the same thing. Someone who believes that he worships the right God in the right way may wonder about other religions. Does the believer in another religion worship the right God in the wrong way, or does he worship the wrong God? How might the question be decided?

The word "God" is often used as if it were an individual's proper name but there are serious objections to this.[2] Philologically it is not so, for it is translated from one language to another, not transliterated. "God" is rarely used as a proper

---

[1] Three collections of papers give the flavour of this debate: *New Essays in Philosophical Theology* (1955), ed. Anthony Flew and Alisdair MacIntyre; *Faith and Logic* (1957), ed. Basil Mitchell; and *Talk of God: Royal Institute of Philosophy Lectures, 1967–1968* (1969).

[2] Peter Geach, *God and the Soul* (1969), pp. 108f.

name in the Bible. The religious situation is complex. Muslims have and use a proper name for God, Jews have one but do not use it, and Christians have no proper name for God at all. They use phrases expressing his relation to the believer, compounded of nouns like *Lord* and *Father* and qualifying adjectives such as *Eternal, Heavenly, Almighty* and *Holy*. In fact, the languages of the religions show a certain hesitation about designating or describing God. A proper name preserves a sense of mystery in that it does not of itself entail any descriptions: its disadvantage is that it carries a suggestion of henotheism. Use of the name "Yahweh" suggests the claim, "We are the people whose God is Yahweh; other peoples worship other Gods". On the other hand, if "God" is a predicable then propositions of the form "God is p" should be analysed as "X is (a) God and X is p". And if the word "God" means "That which is the (proper) object of religious worship" the analysis of "God is p" should be expanded to "the proper object of worship is one who is p". There is a certain skirting about God here, a hesitation about speaking of him or mentioning him in a straightforward way.

The same point is expressed in the classical distinction between two sorts of statement about God. These are negative statements, of the form "God is *not-p*", which come first, and have a certain primacy; and there are affirmative statements of the form "God is p". It is generally thought that all these affirmative statements must in some way link God and the world, if only because the first intention of whatever term or terms are used in the predicate must be secular. Thus in calling God Father one must be linking divine paternity with human paternity in *some* way, however difficult it is to say in precisely what way. There are widely differing views about how much can be done in these affirmative statements and we shall be especially interested in the very strict views held by some theologians.

Many great authorities have held that negative statements provide the only safe way of speaking about God. If one cannot say what he is, one can at least avoid error. It is safe to say what he is not. A well-known authority on the spiritual life directed his correspondent to think about God by excluding all other thoughts from his mind, and perhaps let the cat out of the bag by expressly comparing praying with falling asleep.[1] When you have made your mind a *tabula rasa*, what are you thinking about? It sounds a Zen question.

There is a sort of inference called by Kant disjunctive syllogism, which might be thought relevant here. Its form is "either *p* or *q* or *r*; but not *p* or *q*: therefore *r*". We often use it. For example, if you are driving the car and I am navigating I can get you to our destination by negative directions alone. At each fork, junction or crossing I say to you "not left", "not right" or "not straight on" as appropriate. I can define our course negatively because at each point where a decision must be made there is a limited number of distinct options, from which I proceed to strike out all but one. But the negative theology does not seem to have this form, for in its case what God is is not on the list. The way in which it is said that he is not this, and not that, seems to leave nothing for him to be. It is as if, to return to our driving metaphor, I told you to keep going but not to go straight on, nor to turn right or left. Certainly the negative theology *alone* cannot make it clear whether or not there is anything left for God to be. It does not distinguish theism from atheism.

Thus the classical negative theology cannot succeed by itself in making a clear assertion about God. But we should not leave it for the moment without pointing out that the mystic rejoices in this situation. His message is that theism and atheism are indiscriminable: that is precisely the point he tries to make in speaking of God as Silence, a Void, an Abyss, a Desert, Night, a Shoreless Sea. His journey is a journey into unknowing. At least one very important strand in religious aspiration would prefer to say that God is nothing rather than that he is anything, because atheism is nearer the mark than even the most refined analogical theism. Examples from the theologians are not hard to find. In Paul Tillich's

[1] John Chapman, *Spiritual Letters* (1935), XLII and XLIII.

Systematic Theology occurs the sentence "God does not exist".[1] In S. Kierkegaard's *Concluding Unscientific Postscript* occurs the sentence "God does not exist; he is eternal".[2] This is not a piece of wanton cleverness: long ago Erigena called God "Nihil".[3] It was customary in the great theologies of the past to assert the primacy of the "negative way".

Still, it would seem that at least one affirmative statement about God is necessary, to save theology from emptiness. To make this statement the reference of the term "God" needs to be made clear. How can this be done?

An *ostensive definition* might serve, which could indicate God extra-linguistically by pointing him out. "These be your Gods, O Israel." But in theism direct indication of God is ruled out as idolatry. God cannot be pointed out as one might point to this carpet or that table, or some other topic of conversation. We would certainly not have understood the meaning of the term "God" if we were to suppose that he could be pointed out in such a way.

Alternatively it may be supposed that a *real definition*, in the logician's sense, is possible. But again, this would seem to be ruled out. God is infinite and simple. He has no structure, and is not a member of any class: so that definition *per genus et differentiam* would seem to be impossible, and you cannot construct an analytical definition of God in which the logical structure of the defining expression would be isomorphous with the real structure of the object to be defined.

This reduces the alternatives to either *indirect ostensive definition* or the construction of a referring phrase or set of referring phrases comprising a *description* which clearly can be satisfied by one and only one individual.

By an indirect ostensive definition I mean something like the reply once given to the question, "What is philosophy?" The answer was, "It is what all those books are about." I will mention three proposals to define God in this way.

[1] Volume I (London 1953), p. 227 (Chapter VIII).
[2] Eng. trans. (1941), p. 296.
[3] See Henry Bett, *Erigena* (1925), pp. 96f.

A. It might be said that God is the one addressed in certain acts of worship, rituals and prayers. However, I think it would be quite possible to observe these events taking place and yet fail to understand who it could be to whom they are addressed. The believer himself says that worship may be displeasing to God, the rituals may be empty and idle. Their efficacy cannot be guaranteed by their mere performance. There is no inevitable and unmistakable connection between the indicable outward show and the invisible "inner reality". God is free to forsake the temple, and may do so.

B. It may be claimed that a direct or immediate apprehension of God is enjoyed or may be enjoyed by some or all men, and that this supplies the reference of theological statements. All the subsequent parabolical descriptive phrases are gathered about this point, and hooked on to it. However, there is notoriously an unbridgeable logical gap between the psychological statement that I am enjoying a certain experience and the claim that in that experience God has been cognized. This gap was not discovered for the first time by philosophers. Theologians have long insisted upon it. God is not known by acquaintance in this life, but only by description. Claims to direct experience of him are easier to make than to check. The way God is spoken of precludes any sure procedure for either obtaining mystical experiences or, if they are given, certifying them genuine.

C. The third proposal is that God may be defined ostensively by pointing to Jesus. But it seems clear that all statements about God cannot be analysed without remainder into statements about Jesus. The identification of God with Jesus can only be made plausible if the figure of Jesus is surrounded by and understood through theological notions such as *Son of God*, *Incarnate Word of God* and the like. But these notions themselves already make reference to God. So there is a circularity here. In order indirectly to designate God by pointing to Jesus you must understand Jesus in a way which presupposes a prior understanding of "God".

There can then be no ostensive definition of God. You

cannot point to anything and say absolutely "that is God". If you say, God is the one to whom that liturgy is addressed, the one cognized in that experience, the Father of that man, then you will need theological statements which already make reference to God in order to relate the thing pointed out to God. Pointing to a thing, and saying that it is related to God in some way, presupposes that we know how to talk *about God* and cannot by itself make reference to God possible.

What about the possibility of designating God descriptively by some referring phrase? We might, for example, suppose that the propositional function "X is the maker of the world" can be satisfied by one and only one being, and that being is God. Thus God can be defined as the maker of the world. This image is so homely and so familiar to us that we may not at first see its difficulties. To many people it is far from obvious that the world needs a maker, or that there is any sense in talking about one. The making and dependency supposed are quite unlike other instances of making something or being dependent upon something. It is not clear that the expression "the maker of the world" could designate an individual.

Furthermore, some will certainly insist that God ought to be defined purely conceptually, because he is not only the creator of this world, he would also be the creator of any other world that might have been actual, and indeed need not be creator at all. What God is is unaffected by any particular features either of this world or of any other possible world. Thus the proper definition of God would perhaps be "that than which a greater cannot be conceived and is greater than we can conceive". The conditions which a being must fulfil in order to be God ought to be *a priori* : or at any rate they ought not to presuppose any actual feature of this or any other possible world.

But now we see, not merely that it is hard to conceive of the fulfilment of the condition stated, but that we have entered a realm where all talk of conditions, and all possibility of description, is at an end: and theism demands that this step be taken!

It seems then to be an important matter of principle that God should remain elusive so that his identification must be problematic. Nor is this surprising, because the elusiveness is built into the fundamental rules governing theological language. It was not absence of mind, but calculation, which made things so. If God were not thus elusive he would not be God.

We may deal now more briefly with the question of the logical predicate of a proposition about God. Suppose that a logical subject has been set up for predication. Something is now to be predicated of it in order to make an assertion. Now to make a genuine assertion the function predicated must mark out or delimit a certain range of states of affairs with which it is compatible and preclude another set of states of affairs with which it is incompatible. It must include and exclude, assert that the subject is thus and not so. And it is generally held that theological assertions do not come up to this specification: they do not succeed in being assertions because they set out to be systematically indeterminate. How can it be said of an infinite being that he is thus and not so? If the heaven of heavens cannot contain him how can there be in the world a decisive and adequate expression of what he is?

Of course meaning doesn't *have* to be fully determinate. When placing the fieldsmen the captain of the cricket team may say to me "midwicket" with a gesture. The word and the gesture do not indicate to me one and one only spot on which to plant my feet. He may well expect me to use my own wits in interpreting his instruction, standing on the boundary for the slogger and closing in upon the tailender. But the meaning of what he says is not quite indeterminate either. If I go to square leg or long-on I shall show that I have not understood him as I should have done.

But the vagueness of theological assertions is not of this kind. It is not just that there is, so to say, a little play allowed in the interpretation of them. They are compatible, it would seem, with any state of affairs whatever. God is unchanging and the use of fixed forms of prayer over many centuries and in all manner of circumstances seems to imply that certain affirmations ought to be made about God whatever be the case. You cannot reliably infer from the fact that you are afflicted today that God is either angry with you, or is evil; and nor will you be able reliably to infer from tomorrow's prosperity that God is benign and that you stand high in his favour. However happy or hideous your situation, God is constant in his love, his hatred of sin, his mercy to the penitent.

But now, are propositions about God analytic or synthetic? Theism is surely trying to have it both ways. It wants, however dimly, to see the hand of God in the way things go, but it also wants to say that what God is is in the end independent of the way things go. It seems to advance an assertion, but when it is challenged draws back and changes the assertion into a definition.

Thus it is very difficult to see what it is that is asserted by someone who says that God is this or that. There is at least a case for saying that all he is doing is commending an attitude. But we may, before leaving this subject for the present, remark that attitudes may be reasonable or unreasonable. Even attitudes seem to presuppose beliefs. For I can properly ask somebody "Why are you so cheerful?" or "What makes you so sad?"

Conclusion

We have described two principal objections to belief in God. Religion works through imagery drawn from human life. Inevitably the imagery of a religion bears the marks of the society in which that religion began, so that social change may make the imagery partly obsolete. Furthermore, in a developed scientific culture the ways in which we think about the universe are shaped by mathematics and technology, rather than by personal imagery, so that *any* system of anthropomorphic imagery begins to seem suspect.

But can theology make and justify statements about God which are simply perennially true? Prior to that question is the question whether a clear theological assertion can be made at all, and the answer is that the logic of God appears to be irreducibly "vague".

But this is not a new discovery. There is an old story, presumably based on Josephus,[1] that when Pompey took Jerusalem in 63 B.C. he and his officials insisted on entering the Holy of Holies in the Temple. They were astonished to find—an empty room. In truth the basic logical features of "God" are apparent in the very earliest theistic texts we have. God is invisible; idols of any kind are forbidden; he is in perpetual movement; there is at first resentment at the suggestion that he could be imaged by a king or a fixed temple and he can and does desert both; he may not be tested or tried or "tempted". Theism does not just *happen* to be incoherent or vague: it *is*, it is *defined by* its logical anomalies. The problem should be put like this: does theism defeat itself by proposing a set of rules for talking about God observance of which makes usable, meaningful assertions about God impossible to formulate? How can theism work?

In the first part of this book we shall pursue these problems of belief in God, before turning in the second part to ask whether Jesus Christ can in some sense solve them by presenting God to men in humanly intelligible terms and so tying talk of God down.

For the present, however, we have to consider an objection to our procedure so far. The objection is that the difficulties we have found have arisen because we have misconceived the nature of theology. We have raised a dust and are now complaining that we cannot see.

---

[1] *Antiquities of the Jews*, XIV, 69ff.

2

CONFESSIONAL THEOLOGY

MUCH TALK of God seems to be descriptive, but yet on analysis it appears that it is governed by rules which make a descriptive or "objectifying" theology impossible. There is a realistic strand in religious discourse, but also a strand which says that God is ineffable or incomprehensible, that "God understood is not God".

If by theology we mean a *science*, an ordered body of well-established knowledge about God, then the claim that theology is impossible may bear various meanings.

In the first place, theology may be said to fail because *it has no object*. We might conclude, with the agnostic, that the language of theology is so unclear and incoherent that we do not have sufficient reason to think that it has any object, or we might conclude, with the atheist, that its language is such that it cannot possibly have an object.

Secondly, theology may be said to fail as a science because of *the nature of its object*. It may be that the object of theology is such that assertions about it with a tolerably determinate meaning cannot be formulated. Theology may be subjectively impossible in that our cognitive powers are limited by the bounds of sense and God must be outside their scope, as Kant taught. Theology may in addition be objectively impossible in that God, being absolute, cannot as such enter into the relation to a knower which theology's possibility would require. This extreme view was taken by Mansel[1]—on a strict interpretation of his teaching—who held that specu-

---

[1] H. L. Mansel (1820–1871), English philosophical theologian. See *The Limits of Religious Thought Examined* (1858), Lectures II and III.

lative theology is not merely contingently impossible because of what we are, but that it is logically impossible because of what God is.

But there is a third sense in which it may be held that theology is impossible. It may fail, not because it has no object, or because it cannot attain to its object, but rather because *its method is radically wrong*. It takes up a relation to its object which is such as to exclude its object. There is only one possible relation in which a living man can stand to God, namely the concrete existential relation of the believer to his Lord, and as soon as this relation is, not *lived* but *thought*, objectified—it vanishes. That is, the relation to God exists in the concrete wherever there is a believer: God is present as Lord, the only mode in which he is ever present: but when the relation to God is *thought* God ceases to be present to the thinker as his *Lord*, and therefore ceases to be present. He disappears instantly. The God-relation cannot be objectified in thought.

So it is said that the error of much traditional theology lies in its use of objectifying language, which is to say, its use of a speculative method like the method of traditional metaphysics. There is a dual error—there is the objectifying method, and there is the bogus object posited by the use of it. The theologian attempts to abstract from his own concrete faith, or to conceal his lack of it, and to speak of God dispassionately or objectively in such a way that his statement can become as it were public property. Such a statement is no longer tied to a particular person and occasion: it has ceased to be a particular man's confession and instead is considered as expressing a proposition. The God thus described becomes a kind of hypothetical public object with the odd property of being systematically hard to identify and hard to describe. But this difficulty is factitious. There is not the slightest difficulty in identifying the God confessed in a particular religious utterance. He is the speaker's living Lord. Generalize, abstract, make God into an hypothetical public object and he ceases to be essentially any believer's living

Lord, that is, he is no longer the God of faith. He is prob-lematical. He is indeed an idol. Thus the logical peculiarities of theological propositions are signs of a judgement upon objectifying theology. It has attempted the impossible, and indeed the forbidden.

Søren Kierkegaard saw something ridiculous in "objectify-ing" theology, and his writings abound in sardonic parables against it. It is true, we can see the joke. Consider the follow-ing opening sentence from Wallace I. Matson's book, *The Existence of God* (1965): "The purpose of this book is to investigate the reasonableness of believing that there is at least one god." There is indeed a sense in which that sentence is comic—comic in its profession of detachment, its supposi-tion that the question of the justification of faith in God can usefully be tackled in such a way.

Bultmann on Theology

A particularly clear account of the issues with which we are at present concerned is given by the German theologian Rudolf Bultmann.[1] Like many theologians he distinguishes a sense in which theology is impossible from a sense in which it can and must nevertheless be done after all. But he affirms that theology is impossible in a most thoroughgoing way, and only allows it to be possible with the most stringent qualifica-

[1] Bultmann is not the man to write a systematic theology or philosophy of religion. His ideas have to be sought in the volumes of his Collected Essays, *Glauben und Verstehen* (1933, 1952, 1960, 1965). Many of these essays have appeared in English translation in *Faith and Understanding* (1969), *Essays Philosophical and Theological* (1955) and *Existence and Faith* (U.S. 1960, Britain 1961). The best critical works (with bibliographies) are *The Theology of Rudolf Bultmann*, ed. C. W. Kegley (1966) and *An Introduction to the Theology of Rudolf Bultmann*, by W. Schmithals (1968): see also A. Malet, *The Thought of Rudolf Bultmann* (Irish U.P. 1969), Eng. Trans. of *Mythos et Logos* (Geneva 1962). The account of Bultmann which I give will certainly be called too brief. The question is, in denying that God can be apprehended "objectively" is Bultmann standing in the tradition of those who have talked of the problem of analogy, or is he attempting something quite different? I assume the latter here, but if the former be right then the difficulties and limitations of doctrines of analogy are discussed in Chapters 4 and 5.

tions. He is almost the extreme case among those who say that speculative or objectifying theology is impossible, and that theology must instead be confessional or kerygmatic.

Theology, says Bultmann, was first invented by the Greeks.[1] It meant discourse about the divine, the gods. For the Greeks believed that a rational knowledge of divine beings was possible because they thought of the gods as included within the cosmos. The gods in some way were subject to the same necessities as men and even seemed to share a common nature with men.

But in the biblical tradition we find a wholly different deity, who is in no way at men's disposal and not in any way of a kind with men. He is not available to human thought. He is only available as he is Lord of human existence and his sovereign grace avails. We cannot abstract away from our concrete existential relation to this Lord, so that it might be possible to talk about him as the supreme being. As soon as we try to do so, the Lord disappears. For God is never God the supreme self-subsistent being to us, but only *our* God, our Lord. Both theology of nature and theology of revelation are impossible.

Like Barth, Bultmann is unmystical. God for him is other than man, he stands over against man. But he is not over against us in the sort of way in which an object of thought is over against the thinker. Bultmann uses analogies drawn from human love, trust and friendship. As soon as love, trust or friendship are objectified, submitted to objective scrutiny, they disappear. A man who puts a private detective to watching his wife in order to assure himself objectively of her fidelity will find that he achieves precisely the opposite result: he will not strengthen, but terminate any trust between himself and her. The objectifying approach is self-defeating. It takes up a standpoint which systematically shuts

[1] The substance of the following paragraphs is already present in the 1925 essay, "What does it mean to speak of God?" (*Glauben und Verstehen* I, Eng. trans. in *Faith and Understanding*, 1969).

out the very reality which it seeks. For trust cannot be verified objectively, but only lived subjectively.[1]

So it is also in the God-relationship. Adam's sin was to objectivize the God-relationship by asking the fatal question "Did not God say . . .?" Thus for Bultmann any theology which purports to prove God's existence, or to furnish evidence of his revelation, or to talk *about* God, is atheistic. Bultmann fully acknowledges that theology has to be about God—but as such it is impossible. Talk of God as creator of the world, or as a personal metaphysical being, is idolatry. God is only real for me as I acknowledge that I owe my entire existence to him and live out that acknowledgement.

The traditional theologian may say to Bultmann at this point, "Well, yes, we have always confessed that God is incomprehensible, and every man of faith has felt that the way of analogical talk about him is only an attempt to fabricate an immense idol, which must be knocked down as soon as it is set up: but surely we *can* talk about God indirectly by talking about his effects? If natural theology, or indeed any descriptive language about God, is to be ruled out we can still speak about his effects in the souls of believers. We can talk about what God is for the believing man".

But even here Bultmann jibs. His objection is partly that there is no sure logical route from psychological talk about my experiences to theological talk about what God is doing in me. But still more, I can no more objectify my own existence and talk about myself than I can objectify God and still be talking about him. Or at least, in so far as I have succeeded in objectifying my own existence it has ceased to be *my* authentic existence in faith, and has become alienated from itself. Authentic human existence is not an intelligible essence

[1] In discussing existentialism I use the term "subjective" rather than the term "existential", for which Bultmann has two different words. "Subjectively", in the Kierkegaardian sense, means here roughly "from the concrete individual's inwardness, by an outgoing moral energy". The contrast is *not* the same as that between object and subject in the older theory of knowledge.

at all, but a perpetual coming-to-be in encounter and decision. The freedom of the moral agent is as much an unspeakable mystery for Bultmann as it was for Kant. Indeed, Bultmann says that I cannot even objectify my own sinfulness without its ceasing to be *my* sinfulness.

Thus it is quite incorrect to speak of Bultmann as reducing theology to anthropology. Faith, and the believing man's existence, and the reality of moral freedom before God are just as inaccessible to speculative thought as God himself.

Having thus reduced theology to a complete impasse, Bultmann adds a final, almost mischievous, paradox. If theology is impossible, and if the God-relationship too is unthinkable, must it not follow that the Christian faith is unthinkable, and therefore religion impossible? But to abandon ourselves to silence, to quietism, would itself be a failure to achieve authentic human existence. A theology of God is impossible, a religious anthropology is impossible, and silence is unfaith.

Man in sin cannot, of course, have any pre-understanding of what authentic human existence is: he can only know what it is in entering upon it. But since he does not know what it is he cannot achieve it of himself—it must be a gift. Thus we can be saved only by grace, by a grace which actually brings us into the state of salvation. And, correspondingly, human words can only be in any sense at all words of God by a miracle of grace. The only possible talk of God is talk in obedience to his command that we shall speak. On that occasion, when we speak haltingly, with stammering lips and in a strange tongue, of God, then God the Holy Spirit may take hold of our words in a way we can neither predict nor understand, and make them words from God. Under the constraint of the Gospel the preacher speaks, as he must; but he has no power to make his own words words from God, and he has no way of knowing whether or not God will choose to take hold of his words. It is only apparent that God has spoken when something happens to someone in the congregation. The hearer himself doesn't understand, he hears and obeys. The understanding, such as it is, only appears in the obedience.

The paper "What does it mean to speak of God?" ends with the words "Even this lecture is a speaking about God and as such, if God is, it is sin, and if God is not, it is meaningless. Whether it has meaning and whether it is justified—none of us can judge".

It is indeed not easy to criticize Bultmann, because he is so careful to put faith beyond criticism. But a price must be paid for this manœuvre. Bultmann has elsewhere defined theology—with some inconsistency, perhaps—as "a conceptual account of human existence as determined by God".[1] As such it is preparatory to preaching. It is useful at least in making it clear what cannot be done in preaching, and the spirit in which the task should be approached. Rather as early Christian apologetic began with an attack on idolatry, so in Bultmann's thought the theologian's attack on objectifying theology clears the decks for preaching.

So there we have it. If any utterance purporting to be about God happens to be meaningful it is so only in the particular moment of uttering—hence Bultmann's reluctance to publish his sermons—and in a way which is not amenable to analysis. For as soon as an assertion is abstracted from the particular utterance God has been excluded. No other account of the matter is compatible with the biblical witness.

Clearly there is a factual question here, as to how exactly the biblical writers speak of God. We have agreed that the logical rules for using the term "God" create extraordinary difficulties for theological language. That God is invisible, that he may not be represented by images, that he is free, sovereign Lord, that he may not be tested—these principles, derived from the Old Testament, both define what monotheism is, and seem to make it well-nigh inexpressible.

And it is not accidental that the man who holds these views is the greatest of modern Gospel critics. For they are plainly

[1] Schmithals, *op. cit.*, pp. 46f.

35

related to his understanding of the nature of the preaching of Jesus, and of the preaching that Jesus is the Christ.

And one may agree that in religion there is an attempt, as Bultmann phrases it, to unite subjective truth and objective reality. It is true that the entry of subjectivity into religious knowledge creates peculiar difficulties. But Bultmann's conclusion seems very strange. He seems to reduce God to the God-relationship as if I could enter upon a relation of love, trust or friendship without prior knowledge that the relation has another term. It is very hard to see how the act of trusting can ever be qualified in such a way as to make redundant or improper the question whether there is in fact one to be trusted. The subjective, moral reality of friendship between you and me presupposes that we have first cognized each other objectively as men. Without something like that, how does God differ from the invisible playmate of a child's fantasy? In Kierkegaard himself there is to be discerned an occasional anxiety lest the method of bringing the God-relationship into being by the infinite subjective intensity of faith's passion is the most cruel of all delusions.

However, we propose now to explore what religious utterance is by detailed study of an example.

Analysis of a Religious Utterance

If religion is not consolation in time of trouble it is nothing, so let us consider the words a person might use to comfort a friend who has suffered some misfortune. The words are lame, halting. Perhaps he says something like this: "God is merciful, he knows, good will come out of it, cast your care upon him." By saying some such words as these the speaker performs an action, the action of comforting, or at least offering comfort to, someone who is afflicted. In this sense his meaning is his purpose, aim or intention, what he means to bring about by speaking as he does. He means to comfort.

And even if we do not share, or would strongly repudiate, the beliefs implicit in what he says we can recognize that the speaker means well. We can see what he is driving at. We appreciate that by saying what he has said he has evinced his concern, he has expressed sympathy, even though we may not respond very warmly to his manner of doing so. And indeed we could point out that for the purposes of one who means simply to comfort other forms of words or even a non-linguistic act might serve as well, or better. There are many situations in which it doesn't matter very much what one says, so long as one says something, and there are situations for which words are inadequate. Job's friends were doing very well until they opened their mouths. Do we not justly suspect the motives of those who purport to offer religious consolation? Job's comforters turned out to be accusers. Their comfort, when it came to speech, seemed to be a suggestion that Job's misfortune was well-deserved. They comforted him by a sort of accusation, a justification of his misfortune. Bring in God, and you have the old human itch to prove God in the right and man in the wrong.

But our speaker was willing to take this risk. He wished to do more than offer comfort to his hearer by saying something, no matter what. He said "God is merciful, he knows, good will come out of it, cast your care upon him" and in so speaking he evinced his own human meaning to comfort, but he did so in the form of an affirmation of the comfortableness of God.

But now we have a distinct consideration. There is the speaker's intention to comfort, and there is God's comfortableness spoken of in, and perhaps dimly mediated by, the words used. Maybe the hearer could only become aware of God's concern in and through the manner in which the speaker chose to express his own concern: but still I think the speaker supposes that God *is* concerned, whether or not the speech is successful in expressing God's concern.

So the speaker intended that his speech should not merely describe but express his own concern, and I believe it a mark of truly religious utterance that the speaker similarly intends that his speech shall not merely describe, but actually communicate God's concern. He is doing a little more than recall comforting beliefs to the hearer's mind. He ministers divine consolation. Thus in his utterance he joins two things together, though he is painfully aware of the comical in the way in which he put his own weight behind a solemn affirmation of God's comfortableness, like an ant pushing an elephant. He takes a risk. He risks his own expression of goodwill upon an attempt to declare and express God's good will. In any sort of giving of testimony a man must stake himself, his own reputation and good faith, upon that to which he bears witness.

And of course the speaker's cards can be called. The union between his own comfort and God's which he posits in his speech-act can be broken by his hearer. For the hearer may reply, "Thank you, I know you mean well and I am grateful for that, but what you are saying doesn't mean anything to me at all, I don't know what you're talking about."

And this reply is very disconcerting to the speaker. For his offer of comfort has been accepted in one way—the less important—but rejected in all that matters. His human meaning to comfort is frail and ineffectual: he subordinated it all to an attempt to express the comprehensive adequacy of God's comfortableness, only to find that the hearer preferred his human meaning to comfort, in all its frail simplicity, to the massive abstractness of God's.

The hearer has accepted that the speaker meant well *by* what he said, but he found no meaning *in* what was said. The characteristically religious attempt to testify and indeed make the reality attested present by the very force of the act of testimony, by putting flesh and blood behind one's words about God—this was repudiated. The hearer denied, or failed to acknowledge the act as the speaker intended it, and acknowledged only the bare human meaning to comfort. He would not see the point of the curious device of hiding the human comforting behind an attempt to express and administer divine consolation.

What then has gone wrong? We may say that the speaker has not succeeded in saying what he meant, or we may suggest that he did not really mean what he said.

If we are sympathetic to his intention, and appreciate what it was that he was aiming to do, we may say that the speaker did not quite succeed in "getting across" what he was trying to convey. He did not quite succeed in saying all he meant. Perhaps he could have found some more convincing way of expressing himself, which would have shown not merely his human sincerity but also the human authenticity and pro- priety of his religious mode of expressing his intention to comfort by putting all the weight of it behind an act of expressing God's comfortableness. That is to say, it is very important that the act which purports to minister divine grace shall be a humanly authentic act. Otherwise it is a hollow sham.

Perhaps a better form of words, some other way of uttering them, a happier way of putting it, and then perhaps, thinks the speaker, I might have managed it. He might have man- aged to speak with such "power" that his human meaning to comfort and his attempt to introduce divine comfort would have cleaved together indissolubly so that it would have been impossible to deny his good faith or the verity which he was introducing. In the present case he had not succeeded. His utterance lacked "power" and the hearer reacted by prising apart his human meaning to comfort and the divine comfort. The sincerity of the witness was accepted, that to which he bore witness was rejected.

The speaker seeks to screw up the intensity of the religious utterance so that it cannot fail of its intended religious effect. I don't think it can be done, for even the preaching of Jesus was not as "powerful" as all that. It was perfectly possible to hear him without coming to believe in the nearness of God's kingship, or, to be more exact, experiencing God's kingly presence.

Kierkegaard dreamed as a youth that the god-relationship could be brought into being by working up the subjective intensity of the act of faith. Later he learnt better, perhaps. Bultmann seems to suggest that a religious speech-act only becomes effective by a miracle. But this seems an odd way to talk. For we might point to the way in which a religious speech-act can fail of its effect for lack of *human* authenticity. That is to say, it might fail of its intended effect, not only because the speaker failed to say all he meant, but because he failed to mean all he said. His words were dull and hollow, there was no heart, no life in them. If the effectiveness of the speech-act depends so much upon the human factor in it, it would surely be misleading to say that it is bestowed miraculously and quite unpredictably.

It is beginning to be clear that when we are talking of religious utterance it is not very easy to distinguish linguistic from extra-linguistic meanings of meaning. The word *meaning* has itself, especially in English, an enormous number of meanings. But, to keep things tidy, philosophers like to suppose that when we speak of the meaning of a linguistic expression we are talking of one meaning of meaning, namely linguistic meaning, which can be distinguished from all the others such as cause, implication, intention, reference, function, significance, use and the rest. It is hoped that we can distinguish the *meaning of the speaker* in expressing himself from the *meaning of the speech*, considered as a completed linguistic act. But in a way the whole point of religious language is that it blurs over this distinction. It tries to blur it over as much as possible so that in being convinced by the speaker's human meaning we shall be apprehended by that which he introduces in his speech.

Now consider again the ways in which we said that the speech might fail. First, the speaker might have failed to express all he meant. Second, his failure may have been a human failure, he failed to mean what he said. Then there was the hearer's response: he rejected the theological excess baggage but endeavoured to let the speaker down lightly by accepting gratefully what (in his opinion) really counted, namely the speaker's human meaning to comfort. And fourth and finally, if the act *had* succeeded it would have done so in the first place because of the human propriety and rightness of it. Look at it which way you will, turn it over and over, we seem to be ranking the human authenticity and sincerity of the speaker in his act of speaking as prior to the content of what he says.

The speech uttered, in the perfect tense, the form of words, is nothing of itself. It is religiously valueless and empty unless we are first convinced of the genuineness of the speaker in uttering it. It can't be true unless he is true. The religious utterance appears to get all its weight from the good faith of the speaker. He must mean well, and he can't begin to minister the grace of God to his hearer unless he has a passionate desire to put the whole substance of his own well-meaning behind an act of attestation in which he persuades his hearer that what really counts is God's loving disposition towards afflicted man, and not his own disposition at all.

Even if it is in fact true that there is a good and merciful God who repairs human misfortune, it is religiously ineffectual to say so unless the man who says so is a witness to the truth in the full Kierkegaardian sense. Such a man must be the right man, the man sent; he must speak at the right time, the fulness of time; and he must speak in the right way, not as if his life depended upon it, but because his life depends upon it, actually depending his life upon it.

There is certainly a radical disjunction here. Two people may gossip lightheartedly about love in a teasing and flirtatious way, and neither will be touched. But let the moment come when one of them actually speaks a word *of* love, and the relation between them is irrevocably altered. Things can never be the same again: the shift to a new level of language has created a new world. Is not this the relation between theology and religion? And does not this make it appear that theology is either blasphemy or nonsense? No amount of teasing gossip about love could actually introduce love between the two people, but when one of them takes his life in his hands and makes the desperate leap to speak a word of love, love is at once present in all its terrible power. And similarly theological gossip about God might be continued, and might be mildly titillating, for centuries, but God himself would never appear until, in the moment when a word of God is spoken by a witness, God himself bursts upon the consciousness of the hearer. Theology can toy facetiously with the notion of God, but only religion can actually present him.

But religion still presupposes theology, absurd though theology is
The effect of this study of a religious utterance has been substantially to confirm the account given by existentialist theologians of what it is for a religious utterance to have God-communicating power—with one exception. We cannot accept Bultmann's notion that religious utterance can only be "from God" by a kind of linguistic miracle, if to say this is to underestimate the importance of the "authenticity", or sincerity, of the speaker. And appeal to the notion of a linguistic miracle puts an end to argument, and to theology.

For people go on from here to say that the most that theology can be is grammar: it explicates the deep grammar of religious speech-acts. There is no place for a theology presupposed by, and articulable independently of, religious confession. *Fides historica* must become *fides divina*; after every theological affirmation must be put the suffix *pro me*, on my behalf, which makes it a particular utterance. It seems to follow that this situationalist account of religious utterance leaves theology with no special job to do. It cannot, for example, criticize religion, for it has no *locus standi* for doing so. For God is expressed only in expressing himself; and he expresses himself only in the particular utterances of faith, not in the general statements of theology.

So it is said, but I wonder if this conclusion follows. Indeed my suspicion is that it has the unfortunate effect of making nonsense of the faith whose integrity it purports to defend. Of course theology is not religion, and entertaining beliefs about God is not enjoying communion with God. But I would still insist that for there to be a cognitive experience of God there must be, as a necessary condition, one or more justifiable beliefs about God. Our analysis of a religious speech act has not obliged us to retract the view that beliefs about God are presupposed in religious utterances. The religious man has indeed a passionate interest in their truth, but that is not to say that they are constituted true by the passion of his interest. It is replied that they can only be *known* to be true in the passion of religious interest, and that philosophical analysis sets itself an impossible task in trying to determine their truth in abstraction from the passion of that interest. But I am still dissatisfied with this and would still wish to say that religion's passionate interest is in a truth which is not merely something posited by its own passion and actual only in that passion, but in a truth which is independent of it and prior to it. Faith may enable a man to apprehend an object which otherwise he could not have apprehended, but it does not create that which it apprehends. On the contrary, it is in the last analysis receptive. But faith can only respond to an object which was before it, as being before it, if in some way the prior and surpassing reality of that object can be articulated independently of the passion of faith and then recognized in it. For faith itself cannot be indifferent to the distinction between a God who lives only in the believer's passionate imaginative positing of him, and a God who is actual and is truly apprehended in that passionate imaginative positing. One cannot help suspecting that confessional theology is as much open to the charge of idolatry as propositional theology, if not more so.

There is of course an anti-theological strand in a good deal of religious talk. There is criticism of "propositional revelation". Certainly it is true that there are difficulties—I believe insuperable difficulties—in the notion of a revealed proposition. However, there are two claims here which must be clearly distinguished. It is one thing to say that God does not reveal propositions. It is another thing to say that no propositions can be formulated about what has been revealed. Too often the latter is inferred from the former. It is then said that God cannot be expressed, but only addressed, which presumably means that you cannot speak about God but only to him, confessing what he is for you. And from here it is but a short step to an atheological philosophy of religion, and so to interpretations of faith which make no cognitive claim, no claim to knowledge of what is so. In this way an approach which purported to safeguard the primacy of faith ends by subverting it.

The error has been compounded by a serious fallacy which is to be found lurking even in the pages of Wittgenstein's posthumously-published *Lectures on Religious Belief*.[1] It is the fallacy of arguing that because a belief which is purely factual cannot be called religious, an element of factual assertion is no essential or even proper part of religious belief. The inference is invalid. It is made, and made very frequently, perhaps because of the way in which religious beliefs are often held with a peculiar obduracy or defiance in the face of experience which *prime facie* tells against them. This has led people to presume that, if religious belief is quite independent of the way things go, it can imply no claims as to what is so.

But again, this is erroneous, for several reasons. It is a mistake to argue that because faith is sometimes[2] defiant of facts it is itself non-factual. On the contrary, experience could not tell against faith, or put it on trial, unless faith implies assertions as to what is really so. The man of faith says, the facts seem to be thus and so, they seem to suggest such and such a picture of the nature of things, but it is intolerable that it should be so, things must really be otherwise.

Faith is indeed creative in that with an infinite passion it affirms to be the case what it does not see to be the case, and it lives by the reality which it posits. But it is not self-

---

[1] *Lectures and Conversations* (1966), pp. 53ff.

[2] Not always: it was a weakness of the *Theology and Falsification* debate (reprinted in Flew and MacIntyre, *op. cit.*, 96–130) and other discussions that not enough attention was paid to cases where a Christian believes he has progressed in faith as his beliefs have been modified by his life-experience. Cf. Kierkegaard's account of his developing views about prayer in A. Dru (ed.), *The Journals of Søren Kierkegaard* (1938), extract no. 1287.

vindicating, for the act of positing does not bring into being the object posited, but only the moral relation to it. So faith hopes to be vindicated by that which it posits : and conversely it can fail, not merely by loss of moral courage, but by being erroneous or mistaken.

It is thus incorrect to say that "the strength of religion is its independence of the way things go".[1] On the contrary, it is intensely concerned about the way things go. Sometimes it finds itself confirmed by the way things go, sometimes threatened : but if it were really independent of the way things go it could be neither confirmed nor threatened. It could not be tested nor tried because events could not touch it. It cannot triumph if it meets no opposition.

And finally it must of course be insisted that religious belief has been greatly modified—especially in Christianity and Judaism—by the growth of empirical knowledge. It is no secret that theologians are criticized if they give any appearance of fighting a rearguard action, gradually giving ground : but if faith makes no claims about what is so it is hard to see why the growth of empirical knowledge should have so very greatly altered religious belief in the last century. If there could be no battle, why did the theologians shift their ground?

[1] D. Z. Phillips (ed.), *Religion and Understanding*, (1967), p. 1.

3

ACTION AND SYMBOLISM

IF BELIEF in God makes practical sense, then it ought to be possible to make theoretical sense of it. But, as we have found, it is not easy. In Chapter 1 we supposed that theology purports to make straightforward descriptive assertions about God, but we found that the way in which the basic rules for talking about God are set up seems to make such assertions impossible. At the opposite extreme, in Chapter 2, we considered a style of religious thought typified by Kierkegaard and Bultmann, which insists that objective grounds of religious belief are in principle unobtainable. Faith is without excuse. But the meaning of a belief and its justification are bound up together: a belief which is necessarily groundless is surely empty. The attack on "objectifying theology" was made with the best religious motives, but it appears to empty religious belief of content.

It may be said that I have been working on assumptions about meaning which are too strict. But even if they are relaxed the problem does not disappear.

How do we conceive the limits of meaningful utterance? A limit was originally a definite boundary.[1] It was a strip of untilled land separating two areas of cultivated ground. It did the same sort of marking-off job as a hedge or fence.

Now the stricter sort of logical empiricists used to adhere to a denotative theory of meaning. They held that, in a logically perfect language, the meaning of statements should be as fully determinate as the real states of affairs which they denote. A complete logical analysis of a statement will have

---

[1] G. F. Woods, "Doctrinal Criticism", in *Prospect for Theology* (1966), ed. F. G. Healey; especially p. 82.

as many items as a complete analysis of the state of affairs which it marks out. Where the idea of meaning is as sharp and clear as this, then the limits of meaningful utterance can be marked out clearly. Given a clear boundary (in this case, certain standard and universal conditions of intelligible descriptive discourse) it can be clear whether a certain point falls within it or not.

However, there are serious objections to such a hard-edged theory of meaning. It is strongly reductionist: too much so in measuring the endless variety of our forms of discourse by a single narrow standard. Perhaps the limits of meaningful utterances are more like the limits of the earth's atmosphere, which does not end abruptly, but by gradual attenuation. Perhaps they are like the limits of the visible, which do theoretically exist, but which have not yet been reached by existing instruments. Similarly, we may be able to extend the limits of the sayable some way yet. Is not this what a man of genius does? He pushes back the limits of language, and articulates things clearly which people had previously been unable to express.

So there may be scope for theology to establish its own credentials. It is, as it were, up to it to make sense of itself. It is true that theological statements do not fulfil the conditions for intelligible discourse laid down in the *Tractatus Logico-Philosophicus* or *Language, Truth and Logic*. But those conditions were too strict. If theology alone had failed to meet them then people might not have been troubled; but too many other kinds of discourse were prejudiced too.

We can, then, try to make sense of theology without being unduly constrained by the pressure of well-established and strict standard conditions for intelligible discourse. But theology still has to make sense of religious utterance. Religion demands, it lives by, a solid assurance of the reality of God and his promises, and theology, if it is to be true to religion, must seek some way of representing and stating the grounds of this assurance. It must articulate the *content* of faith, and that must include an account of its *grounds*. It is

47

not enough to say that in faith we are subjectively sure of God, though we cannot be sure of anything *about* God, for it still needs to be said *of what* we are subjectively sure. Faith cannot be an autonomous subjective assurance whose content we are forbidden to specify. Bultmann, paraphrasing Luther, says that "Christian hope knows *that* it hopes, but does not know what it hopes for":[1] but if you cannot specify what religion responds to, you cannot even speak of a response.

Theology must try to articulate the content of faith, but all it seems able to achieve is to put our language about God upon the furthest borders of intelligible discourse. The language of religion is vehement and realistic: for it the knowledge of God is the *fons et origo* of all knowledge, the justice of God the foundation of all justice, the love of God the ground of all love. But theology seems to make most shadowy what religion knows to be most real. Religion lives by the *ordo essendi*, the order of being, it lives from God and presupposes God: but theology, if it works within the *ordo cognoscendi*, the order of knowing, seems unable to find any satisfactory way of stating how this can be done. There are theologies which begin vigorously and confidently from God, but in that case the philosophy of religion, struggling to interpret them, cannot state adequately how they work.

The answer, it is widely and correctly felt, must be sought somewhere in the dynamics of the religious life. The marxist emphasis on the unity of theory and practice no doubt itself owed something to the biblical tradition, and it in turn reminded theologians that in the Bible to know God is to do certain things, to behave in certain ways.[2]

Many suggestions have been made. The prestige of the experimental method led English evangelicals after Newton to claim that religious beliefs can be verified experimentally in the life of faith. "We," they said, "are the true empiricists". The most familiar example, to many people, is also strikingly

[1] Cited by Schmithals, p. 323.

[2] For example, Jeremiah 22:15f.; and the treatment of "truth" in the fourth Gospel.

early. When Nahum Tate and Nicholas Brady made their metrical *New Version of the Psalms*,[1] they found in Psalm 34 something which their predecessors, Sternhold and Hopkins, had not seen:

> O! make but Trial of his Love,
>   Experience will decide
> How blest are they, and only they,
>   Who in his Truth confide.

A long tradition, stemming from Chillingworth and Butler, has compared faith's assurance with the moral certitude of one who commits himself to a certain course of conduct. Richard Hooker was one of the first to say that our assurance of religious truth falls short of our assurance of what we perceive by sense. "If ten men do all look upon the moon, everyone of them knoweth it as certainly to be the moon as another; but many believing one and the same promise, all have not one and the same fulness of persuasion." In fact it is generally admitted that even "the strongest in faith . . . hath always need to labour, and strive, and pray, . . . that his assurance . . . may grow, increase and be augmented".[2]

Now the main empiricist tradition has held that "a wise man proportions his belief to the evidence". So said Locke[3] and Hume.[4] But a group of believers have each the same evidence available to them. Why then do they differ in the strength of their faith? The answer must lie in the moral realm. Faith can be strengthened or weakened by the kind of life one lives. Can it, then, be said plausibly that faith is justified in the way that a self-fulfilling prophecy may be, by the fact that it tends to bring about the states of affairs which it posits?

It is oddly difficult to express this suggestion precisely and

---

[1] Authorized 1696: *editio princeps*, 1698.
[2] Hooker's *Works*, Keble's edition, Vol. 3, p. 577.
[3] *Essay*, Book IV, Chap. XVI.
[4] *Enquiry concerning Human Understanding*, Sec. X (Selby-Bigge edn., p. 110).

very difficult to find any precise expression of it which can throw light on the question of the content and grounds of faith. We shall test a series of proposals. To avoid confusion it must be remembered that these proposals purport to explain the logic of the act of believing, rather than the content believed. The assumption is that if the former can be explained satisfactorily we will be better placed to understand the latter.

Faith as creative

In *The Marriage of Heaven and Hell* William Blake reports that he asked the prophet Isaiah over the dinner-table "does a firm perswasion that a thing is so, make it so?" and received the reply "All poets believe that it does & in ages of imagination this firm perswasion removed mountains; but many are not capable of a firm perswasion of anything".

By its allusion to Matthew 17:20 and 1 Corinthians 13:2 this text assimilates faith to the creative will of the artist who strives to realize his vision. There are many secular uses of the word "faith" which suggest something of the kind. The army will win the battle if its conviction that it is going to win is sufficiently strong. To have faith in the future is to be disposed to act in certain ways which will probably make the future brighter than it will be if we have no faith in the future. The strength of the dollar is largely dependent on the strength of people's confidence in the dollar. The word "faith" is often used to mean "morale" or "confidence".

In many such cases my belief that p can be explained as amounting to no more than a confident expression of intention to bring it about that p. For example, Churchill once made a prophecy about his predecessor as Prime Minister: "History will not be kind to Neville Chamberlain. I know, because I shall write it."

Sometimes we find faith described as a force or a power in religious contexts. In St. Mark's Gospel[1] there is a suggestion

[1] Mark 6:5; but notice that this text is modified in Matthew 13:58, and omitted by Luke.

that popular faith in Jesus endowed him with the power to perform mighty works, or at least that where faith was absent Jesus' power was limited. Faith and prayer have often been thought of as having a kind of causal efficacy, and the newspapers often report attempts to test "the power of prayer" experimentally.[1] Religious practice is full of strange devices for multiplying the power of prayer quantitatively. Large numbers of people are persuaded to pray simultaneously or successively, or to resort to prayer-wheels, candles, masses, and the like.

However, these phenomena are but an example of the striking way in which in the religious life people feel constrained to do things which they know to be objectively absurd. No Christian theologian regards faith as the efficacious or meritorious cause of justification, and the expression "justification by faith" is understood to mean that justification is by grace through faith, or that justification is *impetrated* by faith alone. The formula "justification by faith alone" does not mean that by a titanic act of will heaven can be stormed, but that salvation is pure gift, and men can (at first) do nothing but believe. Far from offering support to the voluntarist thesis, it implies its opposite.[2] The believer cannot regard his own act of believing as bringing its object into being.

The suggestion that faith is self-verifying is open to a whole series of objections. In the first place it cannot explain how religious beliefs manage to acquire meaning. My act of believing presupposes some understanding of what it is that I believe. I cannot make the practical venture of believing p if I do not know what p is. And I must understand p if I am to argue that my believing that p will help bring it about that p,

---

[1] Amusing examples in P. R. Baelz, *Prayer and Providence* (1968), pp. 33ff. That we *are* amused by them shows that we know they are misguided.

[2] See the numerous entries on prayer in Gabriel Marcel's *Metaphysical Journal* (Eng. Trans. 1952) and *Being and Having* (E.T. 1949), especially pp. 76f. Marcel is throughout concerned to deny that praying is in any way like the exertion of a force.

for this is clearly not true for every kind of belief. If I want to argue that religious beliefs *are* of such a kind that believing them helps to make them come true, I must know what they are.

Secondly, understanding how faith "works" could on this supposition make faith impossible. The placebo administered by a doctor works because the patient believes it will work, and does not know that it is a placebo. Once he knows that it is a placebo there is no chance of his recovering his original innocent faith.

Again, the kind of faith here being talked about has a morally very ugly streak of deliberate self-deception about it. William James makes a humorous suggestion that the infallible way to success with women is to have an invincible confidence that one is irresistible to women. One must assume that the great psychologist was making a sly dig at our appetite for self-deception, for only a woman who wanted to be deceived would allow herself to be deceived by such a man, and a relationship on such a basis could only be a silent pact of reciprocal deceit. No doubt most really successful confidence tricksters must more or less wilfully deceive themselves and believe in what they are selling in order to acquire the conviction that makes the trick work. Self-deceit is a complicated business, but it can have little to do with religion, one of whose first axioms is that God is not mocked.

In fact the insistence on subjectivity in religion is dangerous. It could suggest the believer's confidence in himself, a morally repellent notion. It tries to avoid this by asserting a kind of autonomous confidence in the very act of believing, while continuing to insist on the objective groundlessness of this confidence. If this confidence is really quite groundless we are left in an empty fideism, but in so far as any *pragmatic* justification of it is offered it is open to crushing moral objections.

Consider now another suggestion. It is, I believe, empirically verifiable that if a class of young children have a teacher who thinks highly of them and expects them to do well, they will perform appreciably better than a class who have a teacher who thinks them stupid and expects little of them. Thus to some extent the teacher's expectation is self-fulfilling. People do tend to live up to, or down to, our expectations of them. There is, therefore, it may be argued, a real sense in which a moral confidence (or trust, or faith) in people is reasonable and commendable because it tends to bring about the state of affairs which it posits. And, it may be argued, religious faith is somewhat like this, for you have to *believe* God's promises if you hope to see them fulfilled; you have to expect great things of God if you are to receive them.

However, the teacher in the illustration need not be regarded as deliberately choosing to hold a false belief—if such an act be possible. The teacher is not saying to herself "William is stupid, but I will believe him intelligent, act on that belief, and hope to see him become intelligent". The way she teaches could be regarded as motivated by the probably true belief that children progress better if encouraged. No self-deception need be supposed in explaining her conduct.

The conclusion I wish to draw from all this is as follows. It is doubtful whether I can choose to believe something which I know I have no good reason to believe, and even if I can it is still more doubtful whether I ever *ought* to do so. Of course there are occasions when a man may take the optimistic view and subsequently be vindicated by events. It is often an admirable quality to keep on energetically hoping the best and refusing to believe the worst. But self-deception is never admirable. Invincible optimism or "positive thinking" can only supply an analogy for religious faith in so far as any cognitive claims in faith, any element of assertion as to what is so, are left out of the reckoning. Voluntarist theories of faith are obliged to assimilate the act of believing to an act of moral decision. They neglect the element of *assent* to certain claims.

The best example of this is William James, who offered a "justification of faith" (i.e. of the act of believing) in his paper "The Will to Believe", published in a volume with the same title in 1897. Its subject is in fact the right to believe. The argument of this paper is often misrepresented. Set out summarily, it is as follows: Let us call anything proposed to our belief an hypothesis. Now there is in our culture what may be called the religious hypothesis. Its relevant features may be summed up in the following three statements: (1) "Perfection is eternal"; the best things are the more eternal things, they have the last word; (2) We are better off even now if we believe this; (3) "In our religions the more perfect and more eternal aspect of the universe is represented as having personal form". A choice between hypotheses may be called an option. Options vary in character. They may be living or dead; as the choice between Christianity and agnosticism is a living option in our culture, whereas the choice between phrenology and palmistry is a dead option. They may be forced or avoidable: in some matters we must believe or not, whereas in others we may refuse the option. And in the third place, options may be momentous or trivial, terms which sufficiently explain themselves.

James makes no attempt to prove that the religious hypothesis is a live hypothesis. He seems to think that whether it is so or not for any particular person is a question of fact, and that in our culture the option between "one of our religions" and agnosticism is in general a live one. And if the religious hypothesis is live it will also be one branch of a forced, momentous option.

James then argues that where an option is living, forced and momentous, and one which cannot be decided on intellectual grounds, then our passional nature may decide it. We have a right to choose, and to act upon our choice.

Such decisions are made in moral matters, and in matters of personal relationships, and rightly made. Now the religious hypothesis is presented to us as concerned with ultimate moral values, and in the form of a personal relationship. *A fortiori*, then, it is something which we have a right to believe.

James' argument is cautious, and does not profess to

accomplish much. If it is to be applicable, it can be so only if it is in fact the case that the religious hypothesis is a live option in our culture, and that there are no rational grounds for either believing or disbelieving it. The argument will not give missionaries a right to endeavour to make a religious hypothesis a live option in a culture where it is not so already. Moreover, James states the religious hypothesis in a way which assimilates it as much as is plausible, and I would think rather more than is plausible, to a moral principle. And then he says that we have a right to believe it at our own risk. This amounts to little more than saying that in such matters no one is in any position to criticize us, since there are no more rational grounds for disbelief than there are for belief. And James says nothing about how the taking of the risk of belief might be judged to have been vindicated in subsequent experience.

I think I can guess why James is silent about verification. For in moral matters it may happen that whichever option one embraces one will find one's choice confirmed. If I decide that I will trust no one, I will soon discover that I can trust no one. If the primary-school teacher decides to treat all her pupils as stupid, they will turn out stupid. If I choose to live in a theistic world, I will see the hand of God in my life. If I choose to live in an atheistic world, I will not do so. To a great extent we all come to inhabit the moral universe of our choice. Whichever hypothesis we adopt will sufficiently confirm itself. One cannot help suspecting that the appeal to the creative element in faith ends up by leaving everything exactly as it was before. The more religious belief is interpreted in a moral or practical sense the more ambiguous the notion of verification becomes. The more the adoption of a religious belief is seen as like the adoption of a moral principle the more any element of *assertion* in it is whittled away.[1] The will obviously plays an important part

---

[1] 'James is able to claim truth for the religious hypothesis at the cost of stripping it of its intellectual content': A. J. Ayer, *The Origins of Pragmatism* (1968), p. 222.

in the act of believing, but it does not seem right to appeal to this fact in explanation or justification of the content believed.

Symbolism and Action

There is however another way in which we can point to the relation of belief to action which is more instructive.

Our problem has three elements:

(i) Religious utterances unmistakably presuppose beliefs about God. Faith believes itself to be concerned with what is objectively real, over against itself. If faith is sure it must be sure about something, and what faith is sure about must be expressible.

(ii) The basic rules which mark out what theism is seem to make clear statements about God impossible.

(iii) The practical business of religion is transacted in anthropomorphic imagery which believers know to be objectively inadequate, and yet consider very important.

Any theory of religious cognition, any account of what theology is, must take account of these three elements of the problem of belief in God. How is it that religion, in its passionate concern with the reality of God, can set theology an impossible task? How can religion both be sure about God and yet be sure of the inadequacy of all the representations of God with which it operates? Why should belief in God have this strange dual character of perpetually affirming the reality of that with which it has to do and yet doing so in a way which makes that reality perpetually unattainable?

Here is a line of argument to answer these questions.

There was an old heresy in the theory of meaning which consisted in regarding a sentence as like a freight train. Each word was like a single wagon carrying its own little burden of meaning. So it was sufficient to ask questions about the meanings of words first, and you could then treat the meaning of a sentence as the sum of the meanings of the words comprising it. People made this mistake because they were in many cases atomists in natural philosophy, who believed in the old Paduan method of Galileo, the method of resolution and composition. First you analysed the subject under investigation into its component elements, then you gave an adequate account of each element, and then you put it all together again. The error was compounded by the fact that dictionaries are of necessity lists of single words. It was easy to forget that a one-language dictionary can only be used by someone who already understands the language. You cannot teach an infant to speak by handing him a dictionary.

If we are studying problems of meaning, we should begin by treating the sentence as the minimum complete speech-act and ask about the meanings of sentences before going on to ask what each word in the sentence contributes to the performance of the whole speech-act.

But why stop at sentences? Philosophy is always concerned not just with conclusions, but with the chains of reasoning, the patterns of argument, by which conclusions are reached. And in theology above all, to take one sentence in isolation is to falsify what one is dealing with. The art of doing theology consists in checking or balancing one statement against another, and so creating a kind of texture of thought. A passage of argument is more than an aggregate of sentences, just as a sentence is more than an aggregate of words.

And in fact a rudimentary skill in checking one theological statement against another seems to be a prerequisite of any theistic faith. To take an example from Christianity, any Christian should be able to say both that Jesus is the Son of God, and that he is nevertheless not the Son of God as John is the son of Zebedee. And when it is said that Jesus is God's only son the force of the word "only" is not quite the same as in the statement that Jesus is Mary's only son. For Mary might have other sons even if she doesn't, whereas God can have only one like Jesus. To be a Christian, it would seem that you need to be able to make not one but a *series* of statements showing something of what is believed about Jesus.

We may go on to say that this art, of balancing up one

57

theological statement against another so as to convey an inkling of what it is that lies beyond all the imagery, has to be studied by following the actual movement of theological thinking. You have as it were to read between the lines.

Let us try to make this a little more exact by constructing a series of statements about Jesus' divine sonship, and so to say tracing the thread of meaning through them.

Jesus is the only son of God. By this we do not mean biological paternity of the ordinary human kind. Nor do we mean anything like pagan tales of the origin of divine men in which a deity takes human form and impregnates a woman. To grasp what is meant one should begin by thinking of sonship in moral terms. In Israel the bond between a father and his son was peculiarly intimate. The adult son might act as his father's agent, his representative, and was ideally thought of as obedient and faithful to his father's mind. The Israelite king could be thought of as ruling God's land and God's people in the way that a son might administer his father's estates. Thus Jesus might be thought of as God's representative to mankind, God's appointed and obedient viceroy. Yet to speak of Jesus as God's only son is to say more than that he is a man of faith who is in unfailing harmony with God's purposes, for the same might be said of other men. It is to say also that he is God-appointed, and more, that he is in a unique relation to God which may be expressed by using the imagery of generation. What this relation is we cannot say, except by claiming that Christians participate in it by faith. And to call Jesus God's only son is to claim that only through him can men enter upon a relationship to God like his.

In this series of statements a great body of imagery is invoked. Jesus' relation to God cannot be described directly. We do not know and cannot say what it is. But the various statements that are made, with their qualifications, surely mark out an area. The nature of Jesus' sonship is very roughly indicated by balancing up against each other images of generation, obedience, and appointment. How could any attempt at such rough marking-out be made unless the theologian has some inkling of what it is that he *is* trying to say, and some clear views about the things he is *not* saying?

The next step is to suggest that in a system of religious symbols there is a built-in directionality, which must be understood practically.

It may be said that religious symbols make up a kind of pyramid. The gross primary imagery of religion is the broad bottom course of stones, and the successive courses above it progressively correct and refine it. The peak is invisible, veiled in mystery, but the successive layers point up to it. Contemplating the symbol-structure of a religion, and the progress or ascent which it implies, you get a rough indication of where the peak is.

Now the symbol-structure of a religion must be considered together with the ascetical procedures prescribed in that religion. Even in metaphysics a great practitioner like Plato or Spinoza will include within the system the *paideia* or *ascesis*[1] through which the system is to be understood. It is the ascesis of a religion which gives directionality to its symbol structure, showing which symbols are relatively crude and low-level, and which are higher-level. And so an interpretation of the imagery is suggested. For example, a believer may move (and the move is a *progression*) from petitionary prayer to discursive meditation and then from active to infused contemplation. This progression is accompanied by changes in the way God is thought of. The later imagery is less misleading than the earlier. Thus the reference of the symbolism of a religion is given in the actual movement of the religious life.

Such a progression from grosser to more refined imagery is nothing outlandish. It is customary in many disciplines. In learning physics or chemistry the student briefly recapitulates the historical development of the science. He learns classical mechanics before quantum mechanics. Physical models tend to give place to mathematical models.

It is clearly true that some religious symbols are grosser, more obviously anthropomorphic than others. Professor G. F. Woods used to distinguish three main levels. There is physical

[1] Roughly, an educational process or a discipline.

anthropomorphism, as when God's hand or eye is spoken of. There is social-role anthropomorphism, as when God is spoken of as Father, Judge, Lord or King. And there is personal anthropomorphism, as when God's will, his wisdom and his power are spoken of. There are degrees here, and the more grossly anthropomorphic statements are checked and qualified by the less.

But now the accusation will be made that we are practising sleight of hand.[1] What is happening is this. The gross imagery is clearly indefensible by itself, so the refined imagery is introduced to disarm objectors. But the refined imagery is vacuous by itself. An after-image of the gross imagery lingers to create an illusion of intelligibility in the refined imagery, but it is only an illusion. The truth is that the refined imagery approximates to vacuity. Progress in religion is progress out of religion. We are trying to have it both ways: in so far as we still attach importance to religious imagery we keep a slender contact with religion, but in so far as we really know that it is only imagery we have passed out of religion.[2]

Consider a monotheistic place of worship. The architect must design the building, and the believer must use it, as if God were local—as if he is rather more real in the sanctuary than in the porch. But this is absurd, and was seen to be so from the first (1 Kings 8: 27).

Here is an odd situation. The gross imagery and the refined are unsatisfactory separately, so how can it be claimed that they are productive together? Surely the checking and balancing really amounts to cancelling out?

The problem thus takes on a new form. How can the transcendent, ineffable and seemingly empty God of the refined imagery—of the negative theology—be linked to the relative, practical, anthropomorphically-conceived deity of practical religion and biblical imagery?

[1] See Kai Nielsen, "On fixing the Reference Range of 'God'," in *Religious Studies*, vol. 2, pp. 13ff. (1967).

[2] Cf. the popular suspicion that the cleverer the theologian the less he believes.

Theologians have long been accustomed to distinguishing between negative and affirmative ways in theology. The distinction derives ultimately from Plato, was developed by the Neoplatonists, and is made by such early Christian theologians as Basil of Caesarea[1] and the pseudo-Dionysius.[2]

But do the two ways point to the same God? David Hume, in his *Dialogues Concerning Natural Religion* (1779), suggested not. He gives them each a spokesman: Demea represents the high orthodoxy of the negative way, and Cleanthes represents the popular Broad-Church scientist-theologians of the day. And Hume thought that a choice must be made between the two. Most theologians have tried to combine Demea and Cleanthes, feeling no doubt that religious aspiration demands both a God unlike men, sublime and ineffable, and a God like men, who can move the affections and the will. But are the two demands compatible with each other?

[1] *Against Eunomius*, Book I.
[2] E.g. *Mystical Theology*, III, from which I have taken the suggestion that the reference of theological statements may be given by the way they are ordered hierarchically.

4

THE LIMITS OF THEOLOGY (1)

The Quest for Objectivity

IN SOME sense the man who believes in God considers himself to be subjectively engaged with what is objectively real. But the terms "subjective" and "objective" are notoriously slippery, perhaps especially in theology.

In just what sense is God believed to be objectively real? There are four main answers to this question.

In the first place, the believer may attribute to God the same kind of objectivity as we attribute to tables and chairs and fellow men. But this must be ruled out. A person who thought this would not understand the meaning of "God".

Secondly, he may think God real in some equivocal sense, unique to God and wholly unlike the reality of tables and chairs. This is the "negative theology" which we have seen to be practically indistinguishable from atheism.

Thirdly, he may hold that the reality of God is analogically related to that of tables and chairs, but is in some way greater than theirs. This is the classical "affirmative theology", which was usually linked with an hierarchical ontology—that is, a theory of degrees of reality.

The fourth possibility is to say that God's objective reality is such that it can only be expressed indirectly and subjectively. This is the characteristic theology of the period since Kant. Its great names are Kierkegaard and Bultmann, and we have already discussed it at length.

Of these four ways it is the third, the way of the affirmation of images, which now claims our attention. It is the way taken in the classical theories of how analogical knowledge of God is possible. It tries to steer a middle course between the anthropomorphism of the first way, and the agnosticism of the second. It seeks some kind of justification of religious imagery. It holds that God is both like and unlike us: when we speak of him the words we use are stretched to their furthest limits, but they do not quite fracture.

The arguments we have been considering are confusing, partly because the terms objective and subjective shift in meaning. Kant contrasts subjective judgements, which are psychological, with objective judgements about the public world. But for the other Lutheran theologians whom we have discussed the subjective is the realm of the practical, that which engages the will, in contrast to what is public, neutral and open to dispassionate consideration. When the two different ways of distinguishing the subjective from the objective become confused, all manner of misunderstandings can follow.

If we take the view that God's objective reality can only be expressed subjectively, the argument may run something like this: since the human mind conditions whatever it thinks it cannot think the unconditioned as such. But a man *can* relate himself to the unconditioned in action, in that the maxim of his action may be unconditional. The only way in which a man can express his relation to the infinite is by the infinite passion of his commitment.

We have discussed the difficulties of this theology. There is notoriously a piece of sleight of hand in it at the point where a morally unconditional allegiance is transformed into allegiance to an unconditioned object. By exploiting this logical weakness it was possible for Feuerbach to transform Schleiermacher's theology into atheism, and there have been similar transformations of both Kierkegaard and Bultmann.

Consider an act of iconoclasm. The only way in which it can be said that God is infinitely more than and other than some fashionable and popular image of him is by the inexcusable hooliganism of taking an axe to an idol. The idol may be beautiful, it may express the highest aspirations of a religious culture, and the available religious language within that culture will not allow it to be articulated why the idol is abhorrent. So the iconoclast can only say by his act, "Not this!", and if people are shocked and say "Then what?", the iconoclast can say no more. His act is inexcusable because the available language cannot be made to express the excuse. There is no way of expressing whether the iconoclast is an atheist or a transcendent theist. His behaviour is ambiguous. All he can do is create a dilemma, for he would have men decide one way or another. He cannot give any assistance to them, for he cannot express in language what God is. Indeed he cannot, for that would be merely to create another idol. Yet in this case we must ask the impossibly difficult question, how can the iconoclast know what he is doing?

Here is a puzzle, for there are two seemingly incompatible demands here. Religion desires objectivity but it smashes idols. It must have imagery to work with: but it must negate it. The demand of faith for a God who is real, and is a possible object of knowledge, seems to be incompatible with the other demand of faith for a God who is ineffable, who eludes any representation in language or imagery. Could a public, existent deity ever satisfy the requirements of faith?

We see why J. N. Findlay was struck by the way in which faith sets for God a specification which no actual object can ever fulfil, and then indignantly rejects all the possible candidates who present themselves.[1] Indeed, we often meet this paradox. It colours the atheism of Paul van Buren, making it a religious atheism which is dissatisfied with any actual deity and is convinced that an ideal deity is alone adequate.[2] If God is ever actual he will cease to inspire: he must be perpetually receding and never attained, an ideal limit and not an actual limit of perfection. And we meet the same paradox in Paul Tillich's talk of a "God above God".[3]

---

[1] *New Essays in Philosophical Theology*, pp. 47ff.
[2] In an unpublished discussion.
[3] *The Courage to Be* (1952), *ad fin.*

Disagreements about what theology is

The religious demand keeps pushing God to or beyond the limits of thought. It insists that God must never be grasped or fixed in a clear thought. We have here a clue to the puzzling elasticity of theological concepts. And this is why theologians have made such a topic of the ignorance of man, the limits of thought, the unknowableness of God.

In theological controversy the religious demand is often reflected in an attempt to shift the level of discourse, to *purify* religious language. Theological controversy is very often logical, in that people are trying to bring about a shift in the way the concepts are used. Yet the movement seems to be towards vacuity.

Let us illustrate this by an example. Consider a familiar religious concept like "an answer to prayer". What is meant by this? Is it something like a reply to a query, or something like meeting a demand? What are the criteria for calling some event an answer to prayer?

One can imagine a same-level disagreement here. One man may say, you can speak of an answer to prayer when conditions *a*, *b*, *c* . . . are fulfilled. And another man may speak of an answer to prayer when conditions *a*, *c*, *d* . . . are fulfilled. The criteria in such a case differ slightly, but the disagreement is on the same level. Both men *mean* the same thing by an answer to prayer, but they disagree in detail about which events may rightly be called answers to prayer. They both think of the efficacy of prayer in similar ways, but they would "cash" or apply the concept of an answer to prayer in slightly different ways.

But such disagreements cannot long be held at the same level. They quickly turn into something more fundamental. They become disagreements about the sense in which prayer is thought efficacious. It is not too easy to maintain agreement about the meaning of a concept, while differing about the criteria for its application. In practice, a man who thinks it right to pray for rain and a man who thinks it mistaken will be found to have different views about the nature of

65

prayer, and so about the relation of God to the world. One is relatively anthropomorphic, the other is relatively agnostic. Soon one will hear talk like this:

> All petitions should be qualified by the phrase, if it be thy will.
> All petitions are answered, but sometimes the answer is no.
> In the end the only right petition is, Thy will be done.

After these phrases have been bandied about a bit someone will say "I don't wish to produce hard and fast criteria for calling something an answer to prayer. It seems to me superstitious to lay down specific conditions the fulfilment of which assures us that a prayer has been answered. The very absurdity of any experimental test of the efficacy of prayer should be a warning against error here. We are to *believe* that every prayer is answered, but not to try to pick out specific cases as proofs that any particular prayer has been answered."

But now there will be a protest: "How can you claim that a concept is intelligible while refusing to specify how it is to be used? Your concept has become so elastic that anything at all can be an answer to prayer, and indeed in a sense everything is, but no particular thing is allowed to be either clearly an answer to prayer or clearly evidence that it is unanswered. Your belief that God answers prayer has become so nebulous that it is no longer a factual belief in any sense. Anything might, or everything does, vaguely confirm it, but nothing is allowed definitely to confirm or refute it. You profess that it is a great point of principle with you that religious beliefs must not be objectively confirmable, because neither God's being nor his works can be objectively confirmable by ordinary criteria, but one might take leave to suspect that your real motive is a desire to protect your beliefs from refutation."

Thus the dispute about the meaning of an answer to prayer comes to be one which could be called philosophical. I think it illustrates a familiar problem in theology. If theology's basic concepts ever become clear and specific, it is falling into idolatry: if they are refined away, theology falls into vacuity. A vivid personal faith and a pure spiritual faith are at odds with each other. Is there any *via media* between anthropomorphism and agnosticism at all?

It is this problem which we are now going to explore at length. The example of petitionary prayer which we have just discussed illustrates what I believe to be a general truth, namely that theological disputes are always at least partly metatheological: that is, they are arguments about what theology is, and what you can and cannot do in it. If we want to know what theology is about, we would do well to ask what particular theological disputes have been about. So in this and the next chapter we shall work partly historically.

Two writers who are concerned to define the status of our language about God are William King and Edward Copleston. Both criticized full-blown high Calvinism, and their criticisms were metatheological. They did not say that the Calvinists were mistaken about the content of the divine decrees. They did not say, you assert that God has decreed X, whereas in fact he has decreed Y. What King and Copleston did was to say that you cannot talk about God in this way at all. Theology is not that sort of thing. The nature of its language is not such as to permit that kind of dispute.

King and Copleston are representatives of a theological tradition which is neglected today and is, I believe, of great interest. We shall begin by studying the character of Demea in Hume's *Dialogues concerning Natural Religion*. Demea is likely to be familiar, and is intended by Hume to represent this tradition. However, we shall argue that Hume's portrait is mistaken or incomplete at some crucial points, so that we shall be obliged to range more widely to correct and complete it.

Briefly, the problem facing the Demea-theologians was this. They were concerned about the status of the language we use to speak of God. Such language had in the past been described as analogical, and was justified by the metaphysical doctrine that there exists an analogy of being between God and his creatures.[1] With the downfall of Aristotle in the early seventeenth century the analogical predication of terms in theology was deprived of this traditional backing. Anglican theology hitherto had been very conservative, even scholastic: now its language was left hanging in the air. What was to be done? Thomas Hobbes concluded that terms predicated of God are predicated equivocally. He arrived at a non-cognitive interpretation of theological statements. Such language cannot be considered as describing God, but only as expressing the feelings and intentions of the believer.

With Descartes, philosophy began its long preoccupation with sense-perception and the theory of knowledge. Our knowledge of God is mediated by representative imagery which *ex hypothesi* cannot be checked for its truthfulness or adequacy. But it looks as if in our knowledge of physical objects we are in a similar position. For our knowledge of physical objects is mediated by the impressions printed upon our sense-organs, imagery which *ex hypothesi* cannot be checked for its truthfulness or adequacy. There seemed to be an analogy between a representative theory of our knowledge of God and a representative theory of our knowledge through sense-perception. In each case any check of the adequacy of the representative imagery seems to be ruled out. In each case it seemed clear that the imagery could not quite be taken literally: God could not literally have human qualities and physical objects could not literally have inhering in them colours, tastes and smells as they appear to us.

Since the two problems seemed so closely related it was reasonable to hope that a solution of one of them would also yield a solution of the other. It was not only George Berkeley, but a whole group of people, who offered joint solutions to the two problems. Not only to Berkeley, but to all of them,

[1] I use analogy when I call a certain vehicle an *airship*. The appropriateness of this analogical name depends upon an 'analogy of being' between water and air. Both are fluid media through which a vessel can move.

it seemed that the philosophy of perception and natural theology were very closely linked.

Demea

Hume's own lack of understanding of Demea, so near to him in some ways, yet so far in others, goes some way to explaining the puzzlement of the commentators. Hume was a good mimic of other people's styles, as the little series of essays called the Stoic, the Platonist and so on shows. In his Demea we sometimes hear the authentic strain. But more often Demea and Hume remind us of the quarrel between Thomas Carlyle and John Stuart Mill. Mill wanted to respect and to learn from Carlyle, but the truth was that for Mill only a Cleanthes-sort of theism, based upon probable evidence— that is, arrived at by induction from empirical premisses— was possible. Carlyle was disgusted by the spiritual sterility, the philistinism, of such an approach to religious questions. "A probable God!", he snorted, with the contempt others have felt for a theory of knowledge which will allow us only inferred friends. The dispute ended the friendship of Mill and Carlyle.

Hume didn't mind a theological method which was religiously unproductive. On the contrary, that was precisely what he wanted. He needed to show that the religious hypothesis, even so far as it can be shown to be true, can have no consequences of importance to us. Hume wanted to free himself from religion. It is significant that Hume wrote to Elliott to ask for help in strengthening Cleanthes' case, but not for help with Demea. Hume knew how to handle Cleanthes. He felt sure that Cleanthes' theology was unproductive religiously. But Demea's thought is practical through and through.

The Demea-type writing which we can be most nearly sure received Hume's close attention was a sermon by William King, Archbishop of Dublin, entitled *Divine Predestination and Foreknowledge, Consistent with the Freedom of Man's Will* (1709). A copy of this sermon is bound up with all copies I have seen of the English translation of King's other book *On the Origin of Evil*, which first appeared in 1731. This volume was studied by Hume in the first edition soon after it was published, and indeed Hume mentions King in the Dialogues. Apart from the sermon the treatise on evil is extensively annotated by the editor and translator, Edmund Law of Sidney Sussex College. Among the annotations can be found lengthy accounts of contemporary controversies about the analogical knowledge of God which had been occasioned by King's sermon. So Hume must have known of these controversies.

To these peak years of Hume's intellectual growth belong also the controversy between George Berkeley and Peter Browne, and William Law's book against Matthew Tindal, called *The Case of Reason* (1731). Hume knew King and Berkeley. How far he knew Browne and William Law we do not know, though Edmund Law summarized their views for him.

There was then no lack of material to fatten up Demea if Hume cared to use it. In fact the contemporary Demeas were on the whole much more formidable than the contemporary followers of Cleanthes. No one who has read the writings of the physico-theologians from Boyle, Ray and Dereham onwards can suspect them of great philosophical acumen. Their famous books are admirable as natural history and there can be no doubt that when Pamphilus in the Dialogues speaks of "the accurate philosophical turn of Cleanthes" he is using the term "philosophical" in its old sense in order to pay tribute to their scientific accomplishments. I don't think Hume admired the physico-theologians' logical powers.

But what did Hume really think of Demea? The commentators have had difficulty in reconciling Demea's evident desire to frame a concept of God which is religiously adequate with the overall impression that in the end Demea's God is religiously remote, sublime—and empty.

I suggest that the puzzle arises for two reasons. The first is that Hume doesn't really explain why Demea thinks that a religiously adequate notion of God must be empty, and the second is that Hume does not explain how Demea would handle the theology of revelation. To be fair, Hume only professes to be writing about *natural* religion, and in the best examples of Demea-theologies the treatments of rational and revealed theology have to be considered as a whole. Most Demea-theologians express doubt as to whether natural *religion* is possible at all. Reason's empty deity and faith's anthropomorphic imagery must be taken together if one is to see how the religious demand is met, and the problems of meaning are solved. This is true, on the whole, of King, Browne, W. Law, Edward Copleston, Richard Whately and H. L. Mansel, to name a few of the ablest. The Cleanthes-theologians give great importance to natural theology and natural religion, and most of them are close to deism. In the jargon of the day, the Demea party called themselves the party of revelation and mystery, and the Cleanthes party called themselves the party of reason (i.e. inductive reasoning) and evidence.

The resemblances between Demea's position and that of Philo[1]—and indeed Thomas Hobbes—have often been noticed, if not explained. Like Hobbes, Demea has a strong sense of the origins of religion in human ignorance, misery and anxiety. For Demea, God supplies what we need and is all that we are not. His business is not to confirm but to redress; not to endorse human reasonableness, virtue and happiness, but to confound and dazzle them. Whereas for Cleanthes God is only accessible and worshipful in so far as he is *like* man, for Demea God is worshipful because he is *unlike* man, dreadful and incomprehensible. God's being is evident because man—and the world—stand in such evident and desperate need of him. He is proved, not from what man and the world are, but from what they are not and cannot be. God's being is as evident as our need of him: our exigency declares that he must be. It is because religion begins from what we lack rather than from what we are that the negative way must precede the affirmative way. Demea's God is

[1] Philo is the sceptic in Hume's *Dialogues*.

empty in the sense that he offers us nothing that is like ourselves to comprehend; he keeps heart and mind at their furthest stretch.

Demea gives religion precedence over theology. The minds of children should be seasoned with early piety, but the study of natural theology should be deferred until the student has sufficient experience of human infirmity and human woe to appreciate how little can be done in natural theology. It is out of character that he should be given by Hume a form of Clarke's causal proof of God. Clarke was not a Demea. Indeed some Demeas, like William Law, eventually renounced natural theology altogether on the ground that if you allow this strange and presumptuous enterprise to be possible at all you cannot avoid the Deist conclusion. Law in fact argued that Christianity itself is the only religion of nature. Others followed Whately in holding that natural religion should be studied after Christianity and not before.

Demea does not, as Cleanthes and Philo accuse him of doing, renounce the analogical predication of attributes to God altogether, but he cannot and does not attempt to justify doing so, because the discussion is only about natural religion and not about revelation. In fact the Demea-theologians ordinarily grounded the use of analogical predication upon the authority of scripture. In natural theology they were clear that no *rationale* is to be found, for they were empiricists in the theory of knowledge. All our concepts are *a posteriori*, they held, formed by abstraction from sense-experience. We have no direct experience of God, and so no proper concept of God. In natural theology the negative way alone is to be followed. So the natural theology of the Demea-theologians is indeed empty by itself.

Cleanthes complains about Demea on this account; but Demea, for his part, regards Cleanthes as an idolator. Demea certainly regards anthropomorphic theism as much worse than a theism sublime to the point of silence and emptiness. An exalted negative theology is an empty vessel waiting for revelation, it is receptive and humble as Cleanthes is not. A silent theology gives the spirit room to breathe, room to move, something to aspire after. God understood is not God. Given a concrete content, given that he be intelligible, God would stifle the spirit. Revelation gives God a relative intelligibility and has practical efficacy, but the ultimate mystery is irremovable. In appreciating what Demea has to say we should give full weight to his abhorrence of the views of Cleanthes.

However, simply to examine Hume's Demea is not quite to do justice to the kind of theology he represents. The dialogues are conducted on terms unfavourable to him. Cleanthes has a natural theology which is more or less self-sufficient, and indeed a natural religion: Demea has not and will not have.

Both Demea's party and the party of Cleanthes looked back to Locke and Newton: who could not in those days? The Cleanthes party assimilated Locke to commonsense realism, and the Demea party stressed the sceptical interpretation of Locke. The Cleanthes party said that Locke has shown that we know God as well as we know physical objects and each other: the Demea party said that Locke had shown that all our knowledge is relative, and we do not know anything in its real essence: not even physical objects and *a fortiori* not God.

Cleanthes' advantage in the *Dialogues* appears in his willingness to regard theological argument and belief as being of the same kind as other sorts of argument and belief:

> In vain would the sceptic make a distinction between science and common life, or between one science and another. The arguments employed in all, if just, are of a similar nature, and contain the same force and evidence. Or if there be any difference among them, the advantage lies entirely on the side of theology and natural religion. Many principles of mechanics are founded upon very abstruse reasoning; yet . . . no speculative sceptic pretends to entertain the least doubt with regard to them . . . (why should) Philo . . . entertain . . . scruples with regard to the religious hypothesis, which is founded upon the simplest and most obvious arguments . . .
>
> (pp. 137ff. in Kemp Smith edition)

Thus Cleanthes denies any special mysteriousness, any special intractability, in theology. But Demea thinks that because of the nature of its object theology labours under peculiar difficulties. And he would make the point *ad hominem* that if you consider what Newton actually says about his concept of gravity you will cease to think of natural philosophy in any over-simple way.

William King (1650–1729)

To find what Hume has left out of Demea we may turn to William King. Leaving aside the particular issue of pre-destination, King has this to say about analogy in the sermon to which we have referred: Having no direct experience of God we have no "direct or proper or immediate notion or conception" of God. Although the Irish theologians learnt much from Locke they rejected strongly Locke's odd account of how we frame our concept of God. King insists that God's nature, his powers and faculties and the way he exercises them, are all quite incomprehensible to us. We may observe phenomena such as we ourselves could only have produced by the exercise of great wisdom and power, and so be led to represent God to ourselves as wise and powerful. But this is only to report how his effects strike us. We know nothing of what it is in God which produces these effects.

If we turn to Scripture we there find God represented by a bewildering wealth of anthropomorphic imagery. None of this imagery tells us what God is. It is there to direct us, not to enlighten us. Scripture contains the practical principles of religion, not the premises of speculation. No speculative inferences can be drawn from it, only practical ones. The image of God as loving, for example, tells us nothing of what it is for God to love. It only tells us what we may expect, what duty we owe God, how we depend on him, what we may hope for.

> If we would speak the truth, those powers, properties and operations, the name of which we transfer to God are but faint shadows and resemblances, or rather indeed emblems and

parabolical figures, of the divine attributes, which they are designed to signify; whereas his attributes, the originals, the true real things of a nature so infinitely superior and different from anything we discern in his creatures, or that can be conceived by finite understandings, that we cannot with reason pretend to make any other deductions from the nature of one to that of the others, than those he has allowed us to make; or to extend the parallel any further than that very instance, which the resemblance was designed to teach us. (§ 7.)

Why does scripture thus represent God to us? King's answer is fourfold. First, he says that no other sort of knowledge of God is possible to us, at least in this life. What is, and in this life must remain, unknown to us can only be explained by analogies. Analogies are formed for, and may usefully serve, a specific practical purpose. We may represent time on a graph by a straight line and draw useful inferences from it, for both time and the line are measurable quantities. But it would be a mistake to extend the analogy between time and a straight line outside this limited context.

In the second place, such regulative imagery is entirely sufficient for the purposes of religion. It doesn't much matter whether the imagery is taken literally, as by the simple, or in a purely directive sense, as by the learned. Those who *are* much to blame are the scoffers who ridicule the anthropomorphism and the incoherence of the imagery. They are to blame intellectually for failing to understand the status of the imagery, and they are to blame morally for throwing others into confusion.

In the third place, says King, even in our ordinary empirical knowledge we have to distinguish how things really are from how they appear to us. Consider the subjectivity of secondary qualities such as colour. We don't know what light and gravity are, but we can handle these concepts operationally. The practical element in ordinary knowledge should not be forgotten. A man is a biological organism, not an angel wrapped in a coat of flesh. Of course his knowledge is practical.

Finally, King points out, as Hume was to do, that we have no direct perception or concept of ourselves. We speak even of our own mental acts in gross physical analogies. We weigh, penetrate, reflect, embrace, reject, retain and let slip: and, if we look coolly at such analogies, we see how strange they are and how little they tell us; but we can use them without much trouble in the business of living.

So King combines a negative natural theology with a regulative revelation. Together the two meet the paradoxical double demand I mentioned earlier. The concrete imagery of revelation meets the demand for a God who can move the wills and affections of sinful men: the negative natural theology behind it preserves God's ultimate unknowability and mysteriousness. The insistence upon authority, the authority of revelation, links the two.

The approach of the Demea-theologians was positivist and pragmatic. We must do our duty within the scheme of things appointed for us, without rebelling, presumptuously desiring forbidden knowledge, or heeding the siren voices of popular sophists.

And there is a strong echo of Luther—the Luther who insisted that revelation in no way adds to our metaphysical knowledge, but rather transforms our self-knowledge: for God shows us not his essence but his "heart", that is, how we are to feel about him, what we must do, what we are promised by him.

Criticisms of King
In the next chapter we continue the exploration of this type of theology. Let us now name some of the principal objections to it.

In the first place, even if you understand revelation entirely directively or regulatively, you are not thereby exempted from the need to systematize it. How can the moral life be coherently directed except by a coherent body of moral principles? The Demea-theologians were trying to ward off biblical criticism. King says that it is a mistake to oppose different images of God to each other, and find a problem in the fact that Scripture portrays God both as foreordaining the future and as calling men to repentance—and even as repenting himself. But there has to be some systematization even if Scripture is to do no more than to direct the moral life.

Secondly, on King's account our knowledge of God is pruned away to vanishing point. Scripture represents God as ordaining the future and man as morally free. If you ascribe any descriptive force to such representations a *prima facie* contradiction must arise. If King refuses to let it arise then revelation is wholly directive and not at all informative. The representation of God as ordaining the future will be compatible with any state of affairs whatsoever. But if so, how can it guide, and not misguide, our expectations? The representations of God as hating and punishing sin, rewarding virtue, and accomplishing his purposes surely lead us to expect some things to happen rather than other things to happen. How can Scripture rightly claim to direct us, how can we rightly accept direction, unless the directions suggest well-founded expectations as to what is and will be the case?

Thirdly, it was widely objected to King that the possibility of religion presupposes some moral community between God and man. Surely religion must be a response to what God is, not a response to regulative imagery?

Finally, have we two gods here? If one distinguishes the ineffable, empty deity of the contemplative's aspiration from the relative anthropomorphic deity of the active life, how can one ever link them again? How on King's account can the authority of revelation as emanating from God be established? Is the whole structure too frail to stand? King offers a solution to our problem in that he shows how faith operates with imagery which is *practically* useful while at the same time conscious that it *is* only imagery and that God himself remains veiled in mystery. It is an elegant solution, but is it adequate?

5

THE LIMITS OF THEOLOGY (II)

Peter Browne (c. 1665–1735)

IT'S AN odd paradox of religion that it demands a God who is both like us and unlike us. Like us in that only a God who can enter into reciprocal personal relations with us, who in some sense takes human form and can be expressed in human terms, can inspire the religious affections and the moral life. Yet religion also demands that all this be negated in the name of a God unlike us, the unknowable absolute who is the never-attained goal of the contemplative's aspiration, for whom the soul perpetually hungers.

Many forms of theism are bipolar, contrasting God abstract and God concrete, God in himself and God in relation, God unknowable and God made known. It is perhaps unavoidable. But there is certainly a problem in relating the two poles.

Peter Browne was Fellow and then Provost of Trinity College, Dublin, and later Bishop of Cork. He introduced the study of Locke's *Essay* in Dublin soon after it was published and anticipated some of Berkeley's criticisms of Locke's theory of knowledge. He tried in some points to correct and strengthen King.

Browne[1] makes it clear that the Demea-tradition's account of analogical predication is very different from the old scholastic doctrine of the analogy of proper proportionality. For Browne, analogy is not a relation of two relations. In the scholastic doctrine there is a propor-

---

[1] See his books, *The Procedure, Extent and Limits of the Human Understanding* (1728), and *Things Divine and Supernatural conceived by Analogy with Things Natural and Human* (1733).

tionality, a *ratio*, an *analogia* between the way God is *p* and
the way a man may be *p*. This proportionality is founded
upon the analogy of being—that is to say, the analogical
predication of terms was justified because there was an
ontic analogy between the being of God and the being of
a man which could be expressed metaphysically.

But Browne rejects this, as Karl Barth was later to reject
it. God and the creature cannot be compared, or be treated
as fellow-members in a class. They are in no sense two of a
kind. So Browne, like Barth, replaces the *analogia entis*
with an *analogia fidei* resting not upon metaphysics but upon
the authority of revelation. This analogy of faith is a relation
among four terms, of which two are unknown; so that it
cannot yield speculative understanding. For example, we
are to believe upon the authority of revelation that there
is in the unknown God some incomprehensible perfection
really correspondent with what love is in men. For practical
purposes we are commanded to think of God as loving with
a human love and to respond accordingly. We are wise,
it is right, so to think of him. But Browne insists that there
is no possibility of thinking an infinite love. We do not
have the transformation-rules for converting our notion of
human love into an adequate notion of divine love. No,
the truth is that we are stuck with human love, it is all we
can understand, and we must take it as it is as an analogy
of divine love. As such it is not informative, but by way
of compensation it is full of practical use.

So the new interpretation of analogy implies a change in
the logical status of theology. It is no longer intertwined
with metaphysics; instead we have a positivism of revelation.
If King looks back to Luther, Browne looks forward to Barth.

How then may we be sure that God does not deceive us?
Browne relies on the authority of scripture—though it is
hard to see how he could establish it—but he does not rely
solely upon it. He points out that we know what the limits
of thought are—a strict empiricist theory of knowledge
makes them clear to Browne—so that we can see why there

is no other possibility of religious knowledge. And we *can* understand the practical effectiveness of such analogies. And after all, the analogies themselves are mundane, and perfectly straightforward.

Browne appeals to commonsense, too. We have no reason to suppose that our ordinary perceptual representations mislead us; on the contrary, they serve us perfectly well in common life. We can operate practically with our ideas of colour, taste and sound, though we don't know what corresponds to them in things themselves: and similarly we can operate practically with scriptural ideas of God. Unfortunately Browne does not suggest how we are to judge between rival alleged revelations *each* prompting a certain way of life, but I think he would have claimed, as Joseph Butler and H. L. Mansel claimed, that Christianity is peculiarly well-adapted to human nature. It alone unites or tries to unite the highest transcendent theism with a God who presents himself to men in human terms.

Browne clarifies King's account of analogy, but the question still remains: if in rational theology theism as distinct from atheism cannot be established, how can the authority of revelation as emanating from God be established? And if you distinguish the sublime empty God of the negative theology from God as he appears in the regulative imagery of revelation, how can you link the two? There can be no non-symbolic statement linking the symbolism to its supposed real referent. He is beyond the reach of language.

Edward Copleston (*1776–1849*)
Edward Copleston was the senior member of the group commonly known as the Oxford Noetics, having become Provost of Oriel College in 1814. It is suggested, I know not with what justice, that the revival of logic at Oriel and the flavour of the Noetic theology owed something to Blanco White, who had undergone a seminary training, and introduced his colleagues to some of the logical weapons of the schoolmen.

Copleston disliked Calvinism, which had been revived by the Evangelical movement, and in 1821 he published *An Enquiry into the Doctrines of Necessity and Predestination*. In this book he writes in the spirit of an earlier Oriel man, Joseph Butler, a spirit much more friendly to Luther than to Calvin. The high dogmatic strain is not for Copleston. The Christian gospel is ordered not towards speculation but towards obedience. It is not for us to speak of, or profess to know, God as he is in himself. Copleston adds a long note on analogy, quoting with approval William King's sermon.

Richard Whately, a young fellow of Oriel, was encouraged by this to issue a reprint of William King's sermon, with preface and notes. It was entitled *The Right Method of Interpreting Scripture, in what relates to the Nature of the Deity, and His Dealings with Mankind, Illustrated in a Discourse on Predestination by Dr. King* (1821).

King's sermon proved as contentious as it had been a century before when people felt that its original audience, the Irish House of Lords, was a hint of something fantastical in it. The controversy which followed has never been studied, so I shall give a very brief resumé of it.

Copleston's book was noticed by Dugald Stewart in the *Edinburgh Review* for October 1821, and both books were dealt with at length in a review article in the *Quarterly Review* for the same month.

Next year (1822) two pamphlets in reply appeared: *A Letter to Edward Copleston D.D.* by "Philalethes Cantabrigiensis", and *Vindiciae Analogicae* by E. W. Grinfield, whose hostility to Copleston was well known. W. Dalby, of Exeter College, replied with a *Defence*, and Copleston replied to what had been said so far in a pamphlet called *Remarks upon the Objections made to Certain Passages in the Enquiry*. Still in the same year Grinfield fired back with *Vindiciae Analogicae Part II*.

Copleston wrote little, and for further material we have to look to the many admirable books of Richard Whately.

For our purposes we need do no more than ask what of material value Copleston and Whately have to say about our present question.

Copleston and Whately continue the Demea-tradition in seeking an explanation of the use of analogical predication in theology which does not presuppose an analogy of being between God and man. But they by no means agree with Browne. They are closer to the scholastics, for they maintain that an analogy is a resemblance of relations. But the existence of an analogy is no ground of itself for asserting any resemblance between the terms.

For example, a proposition may be called the *basis* of a system. That is, its relation to the system is analogous to the relation between its foundations and a building. The proposition *supports* the system, which *rests upon* it. But a proposition and a foundation are quite different entities. We are not likely to fall into the error of supposing that propositions have to be excavated or that foundations are of subject-predicate form. The analogy between one relational property of a proposition and one relational property of a foundation supplies of itself no warrant for inferring any further similarities between the terms.

But where a predicate is attributed by analogy to two terms which *do* resemble each other, or might mistakenly be thought to do so, there are rich possibilities of confusion. Let us consider in turn the ascription of moral qualities to our fellowmen, and to dogs.

All moral qualities, says Copleston, are predicated analogously. The reason is that a moral quality is not a thing, an essence present in, or property possessed by, every man who has it in a univocal way. A moral quality, like courage, is a class name for a large group of relations between particular men and particular bits of their behaviour. A soldier risks his life on the battlefield, Socrates calmly drinks the hemlock, a statesman refuses to court popularity, Penelope keeps her suitors at bay. The persons are different, the acts are different; but there is a family-resemblance, an analogy between the relation of each person to his circumstances. Each may be called courageous. Courage is not an essence univocally present in each courageous person, but a family resemblance running through a class of particular personal acts.

And how do we discover it? We do so by an effort of empathy. We feel what it would be like for ourselves to be in the situation of Socrates, Penelope and the others, and to act as they did. Judgements as to the morality of an act depend upon the connaturality of the judge and the subject of his judgement. It is because we are of a kind with Socrates and Penelope that we can attempt to put ourselves in their place and feel as they felt. Thus the analogical predication of moral qualities is a special kind of analogical predication. The judge and the subject of his judgement resemble each other, and the one who judges uses his own nature, and his imaginative powers, to assist him.

Now consider the case of dogs. Men and dogs are both animals. Dogs are sometimes analogically described as faithful or courageous because there are bits of canine behaviour which resemble bits of human behaviour which we would confidently describe as faithful or courageous. There is no great harm in calling Tray, a dog, faithful or courageous provided that we remember that dogs are different from men and that we must not conclude that the fidelity and courage of a trained dog are like those of men. If we say that Tray is courageous and faithful to his master, we are saying how a bit of Tray's behaviour strikes a *man* who contemplates it. Within limits such talk is not purely fanciful; indeed, it is informative. It implies that if his master is assaulted Tray may be expected to behave in certain ways. But Tray must not be supposed to be a moral agent or to possess moral qualities, like a man. The limits of such language must be remembered, or one falls into the pathetic fallacy.

Now, what about the knowledge of God? Paley had made

the mistake of supposing that God's moral qualities may be inferred from a bare inspection of the natural order. This is not so. Moral qualities are never inferred by such a bare inspection. Indeed, if one were attempted it would more likely lead "to the conclusion that the Deity was a being of a mixed or capricious nature", says Whately, echoing Hume.[1] Paley is wrong, for the truth is that we bring our own moral nature with us when we scan the world for traces of God's workings.

The situation is as if "a tasteful architect and a rude savage" stood side by side "contemplating a magnificent building, unfinished or partly fallen to ruin" (Whately/King, p. 121). The architect, with the knowledge he brings, understands something at least of what he sees. He sees something of what the builder intended, and of the respects in which his intention is as yet unfulfilled or has been frustrated. The savage can see nothing of this.

Similarly, as we scan the universe for the traces of God's working, we do so as men, as moral beings, and on that ground alone are we able by an imaginative projection to discern in the works of God something analogous to what in our own effects would be thought to be manifestations of wisdom and goodness.[2]

There is a similarity of relations between God's production of effects and ours. But such representations of God are relative to ourselves: they express our *human* response. We must not make the mistake of inferring from this fragile base any similarity between the terms, between ourselves and God. God's dealings with men may, for the purposes of religion, be represented as like the dealings of a just and gracious king with his subjects. But we cannot infer from this that God himself is just and gracious in the way that a man may be. For God is very different from man.

[1] Whately/King, p. 121.
[2] This version of the argument from design recalls Gassendi. Whately and Copleston may have known his writings at first hand, or have gathered a hint from Robert Boyle.

We do not have the connaturality with him which is essential if we are to make reliable moral judgements about his workings. So in natural theology Copleston would be as cautious as Philo in Hume's *Dialogues*. But he goes beyond Philo in arguing that our notions of God can legitimately be used to guide our conduct. It is true that to call a dog faithful is not to say anything about his "inner" moral nature, but it is to suggest definite expectations about his behaviour. So to call God gracious or just is not to say anything about his "inner" moral nature, but it can guide our conduct and suggest expectations to us.

"Affectus in Deo denotant effectum," says Copleston (*Enquiry*, p. 103). And Whately—echoing Bultmann, to our ears—warns that "it was the craving after forbidden knowledge which expelled our first parents from Eden". So Copleston quotes Luther: "To know anything of God otherwise than as revealed in Scripture—what his nature is, what he does, what he wills—belongs not to me. My business is to know what are his precepts, his promises, and his threatenings." There is a very important point here. At least in England, the Reformation principle of the sufficiency of Scripture was taken to mean that the relative and practical imagery of Scripture is all we can have and all we need. Chillingworth's famous saying that "The Bible and the Bible only is the religion of Protestants" meant that with all its incoherences and metaphysical insufficiencies the Bible is sufficient for salvation. It is a book to be obeyed, not understood, and in religion it is obedience that counts. If metaphysical certainty in matters of religion were to be had, it would be morally pernicious.

Terms applied to God, then, "are the best means, indeed the only means we have of expressing our thoughts on this subject at all, and they ought never to be used without a reverential sense of their imperfection—and the rule of always interpreting them as *relative* to ourselves is an admirable preservative against many mistakes and perplexities, into which men are led by a critical analysis of scriptural terms. It is to teach *us* how to feel and act towards God, not to explain *his* nature, that such words are chosen".[1]

It is not surprising that this account of analogy caused some perplexity, able though it is. Copleston goes a long way in insisting upon the practical and anthropomorphic character of our response to our environment. I look up to see how a buttress or column supports a building, and I imagine myself supporting it, I *feel* the stresses and strains, and if the column is leaning or buckling I *feel* the need to reinforce it. Our response to architecture is shaped by the architecture of our own bodies, and our response to machinery by our own musculature. I look at the sea, and I talk of it as placid, as cleansing with a priestlike ablution, as now becoming restless, turbulent, furious, raging, and then abating its anger to a heavy swell, subsiding, becoming calm, peaceful, tranquil, benign, smiling. And this imaginative anthropomorphism is not wholly feigned. It has conduct-guiding value. If I describe the sea as becoming restless, sails had better be taken in and hatches battened down. As much as Hobbes or Hume, or indeed Freud, Copleston is saying that religion does not originate in speculation. It springs from human emotional need, our human desire to make human sense of the unknown powers that be, our hopes and fears. We must think of God in human terms, though such terms, Copleston insists, are always inadequate. But, in that case, how can you assert a special authority in one set of human terms, namely those of the Christian revelation? Why does one set of terms have a unique title to guide conduct?

For, says Grinfield, if there is no connaturality between God and ourselves, and if the language ascribing goodness, justice and love to him is not founded in his nature but is merely relative to ours, whence can such representations of him derive their *authority*? How is God to be imitated, how is there to be reciprocity between God and man if an opaque and impenetrable screen of imagery is inter-

[1] Copleston's *Enquiry*, pp. 96f.

posed between them? Are we imprisoned in our own humanness? The incarnation of the Son of God, his atoning death, and the inward assistance of the Spirit all pre-suppose the sympathies and likenesses between heaven and earth which Copleston has denied. Resemblance of effects, by Copleston's own admission, is not enough to found the analogical predication of moral attributes upon. For religion is a moral relation between God and man, and it pre-supposes some connaturality—Grinfield's own expression is "congruity of nature"—between them. If I see another man's act, and project myself into it imaginatively, and then frame a moral judgement upon it, my ability to do this presupposes our connaturality. And similarly, if I am to call God's works good, and to worship him I *either* do so justly because there is a connaturality between us, *or* I fall into the pathetic fallacy. There is no mid-way.

And the reply to this objection takes us back to our original dilemma. If practical religion presupposes con-naturality between God and man, contemplative religion, and indeed the ground-rules of theism, must deny it. If we need, at one level, a god who is like us, we need still more a god who is unlike us, whose thoughts are not our thoughts, whose ways are not our ways.

Mysticism

Cleanthes, in Hume's *Dialogues*, accuses Demea of being a mystic, and of renouncing all analogy. In Part IV he says "How do you MYSTICS, who maintain the absolute incomprehensibility of the Deity, differ from sceptics or atheists . . .?" In Part XI he says, "if we abandon all human analogy, as seems your intention, DEMEA, I am afraid we abandon all religion. . . ."

We can now, I think, estimate the justice of these charges. With regard to analogy, Demea-theologians have been pre-occupied with the subject since the seventeenth century. Demea himself in the *Dialogues* evidently uses analogical language, but the general aim of the Demea-theologians has been to produce a religiously workable account of analogy which did not presuppose any analogy of being between God and man. Philosophically the Demea-theologians were more of a positivist and empiricist turn of mind than of a metaphysical. They all insisted upon the "infinite qualitative difference" between God and creatures. They wished to check the presumption of an over-confident natural theology.

But here they ran into a ludicrous paradox which has long been a source of embarrassment to Christian theologians. Roughly it is that they wanted a bare minimum of natural theology, but not too much.

They needed a bare minimum, in order to create a space for revelation and, as it were, to be able to hook it on to something. It is not very easy to maintain that revelation is autonomous. If you understand revelation to be a system of moral directives which order the believer's will and affections, and then say that these directives are so morally good and efficacious that the revelation must emanate from God you are *either* arguing in a circle, justifying revelation by moral criteria derived from it, *or* you are making your appeal to moral knowledge which we possess prior to and independently of revelation, and so are well on the way to making revelation redundant. Neither of these alternatives is very happy for a theologian.

And with regard to God, if you assert the sufficiency of Scripture and acknowledge the anthropomorphic character of Scripture's images of God, how can you defend the authority of the scriptural imagery except by invoking some rational and less anthropomorphic knowledge of God, a kind of knowledge surely superior to what scripture provides?

Thus, either way there is a dilemma. The moral authority and God-givenness of revelation can only be defended by invoking something external to revelation. But once you have that bit of external knowledge of God, it will surely squeeze out revelation.

Mansel discovered and struggled with this problem.

William Law discovered it, and tried to escape it by forsaking natural theology for mysticism. In general the Demea-theologians have argued, with Butler, that our natural knowledge of God is no better than our knowledge through revelation. Our natural knowledge of God is also imperfect, relative to us, practical, and so it cannot be used to overthrow revelation. Or they have argued that in natural theology one treads only the negative way and that revelation alone opens up the affirmative way. Thus they have been willing to acknowledge that in natural theology nothing is sufficiently clearly grasped to distinguish theism from atheism. The most natural theology can do is to clear a blank wall on which revelation's picture can be hung. In this they agreed with the mystics, who have also been indifferent to the charge of atheism. Neither in natural theology nor in revelation is objective certainty to be had but only subjective, probable or moral certitude. No clear descriptive discourse about God is possible, and there is no way of affirming clearly and intelligibly God's objective reality. But this does not matter, because a probable or moral certitude is sufficient for the purposes of religion.

But now, what of this strange accusation of mysticism? What does it mean? For Hume, mysticism seems to have meant a strong assertion of God's incomprehensibility. The Demea-theologians have as a rule expressed dislike of mysticism, but what they rejected was any sort of claim that there is a special supernatural way of knowing which makes immediate apprehension of God possible. Mansel, for example, cordially detested any such claim, considering it rationally indefensible and subversive of true religion. Any direct acquaintance with God would make revelation's relative imagery redundant, and generate a dualistic piety which would forsake the love of our fellow-creatures for the cultivation of private ecstasies.

The Demea-theologians are mystical in Hume's sense, perhaps, but not in the sense they themselves rejected, with the exception perhaps of the later William Law. For mysticism has very commonly been associated with neoplatonic meta-physics. God is at the top of the ladder of being, which is also the ladder which the soul ascends. In the ascent the soul enters gradually into a kind of void. All imagery, all intelligibility, all knowledge, all distinction of subject and object are stripped away by degrees. The mystic's mind is blank and still, and he has lost track of time and of himself. God is nothing, non-being or beyond being: the mystic is no more concerned to think God through a concept than is a Buddhist.

In such a condition knowledge is at an end, and the only way in which the mystic can refer his condition to God is *by pointing to the direction in which he was travelling when the last landmarks were left behind*. And this is where the hierarchical ontology comes in. God is the incomprehensible limit of an actual series. Since the series is actual, and it points in a specific direction, it must, it was thought, have an actual last term from which it depends and in which it is consummated. As the soul climbs the ladder, more and more must be left behind. When all is lost—knowledge, virtue, love—the soul has reached a condition where it cannot *know* that it has attained the limit of the series. It can only know this retrospectively, on returning to normal consciousness, by as it were pointing in the direction in which it was moving when the last landmarks were left behind, and from which it has come.

When the process of elimination is complete only God *can* remain. There's the necessity, that's why Anselm's *Proslogion* is in the form of a prayer. For what remains when the limits of thought are reached and yet surpasses those limits *must* be God. But nothing can be said about him except by recapitulating the ascetical procedure, by saying what must be repudiated in order to approach him. The negative way, with its ambiguity, must be followed.

Now the Demea-theologians did not have such an hierarchical ontology. Nor did they have an hierarchical symbol-structure, which might have done the job. They were prone to argue, mistakenly I believe, that all human representations of God are on the same level. They maintained this partly out of a respectable protestant dislike of any double standard or hierarchy of degrees of proficiency among the regenerate, and partly out of suspicion that if the imagery of scripture is admitted to vary in authoritativeness or adequacy the pass would be sold to the biblical critics. Both these reasons are unsound. Even in the very earliest Christian ascesis there was an important distinction between "milk" and "meat" stages, and the religious life cannot move at all unless the religious symbols guiding it be arranged, as they plainly *are* arranged, in some kind of hierarchy.

The nearest we can get to indicating the referent of theological discourse from within is by pointing to the ascetical procedures of religion or to their reflection in the hierarchy of religious symbolism. In the old hierarchical ontology it was felt that since the ladder was actual it must as it were have a top rung. It was believed that you could state that God exists, even though you could say nothing about him: *quid est*, but not *quod est*. In my opinion that ontology itself cannot be stated clearly and must be repudiated. If its function is taken over by a symbol-hierarchy it is clear that the objective uncertainty is increased.

In these last two chapters we have used some little-known episodes in the history of Anglican thought to illustrate the incompleteness of rational theology, and the difficulty in completing it by appealing to revelation.[1] The classical doctrine of *analogia entis* was too crude, for it tried to find a middle way between anthropomorphism and agnosticism, and theism is not such a middle way; it encompasses both. The "Demea-theologians", as we have called them, saw this, and their attempts to grapple with the problem are still of great interest. It is not that theism cannot solve its

[1] See also my articles in the *Journal of Theological Studies*, "Mansel's Theory of Regulative Truth" (N.S. Vol. XVIII Part 1, April 1967), and "The Doctrine of Analogy in the Age of Locke" (N.S. Vol. XIX Part 1, April 1968).

antinomies, but rather that it would be a distortion of theism to suppose that there can be any simple resolution of them: God must be spoken of, yet he cannot be spoken of; he must be of a kind with men if religion is to be possible, yet creator and creature can in no sense be two of a kind.

But can Christ, as many theologians claim, resolve these antinomies?

Part Two:

THE STRUCTURE OF BELIEF IN CHRIST

6

THE SCANDAL OF PARTICULARITY

WE TURN now to discuss Christ, under the general title, *The Structure of Belief in Christ*. This development of our theme may arouse some suspicion. There is a feeling that though the philosophy of religion may concern itself with God—it has some historical title to do so, and can hardly be prevented now—it ought to be discouraged from encroaching upon the territory of Christology. Belief in God is in some form common to most religions, it has a certain universality, and it is inevitably bound up with the question of the possibility of metaphysics. It positively invites philosophical attention. But philosophy never makes sense of Christ. Surely the Incarnation of God in Christ is "uniquely unique", and so simply not available to philosophical understanding and criticism. It is a reality which discloses itself only to faith and discipleship. Only the insider can understand its language, and the outsider's questions are invariably ill-framed and merely go to show that he *is* an outsider.

No one can deny the peculiar intractability and awesomeness of Christ and the Christian language about him. But I still wish to argue that the time has come for the philosophy of religion to attend to Christology. The claim that only insiders can really understand its language has corollaries which Christians themselves would surely not wish to accept. For if you hold that some esoteric jargon is and must be kept private to insiders, then you rob it of any public significance and reduce it to the status of a device for consolidating the group.

Now some uses of religious language do look very like the exchange of passwords. By producing the password a man shows that he is a bona fide member of a group. If he can handle its esoteric jargon, and knows the rituals, he proves that he is "one of us". Freemasonry looks—to an outsider—like this. It is important to know the jargon and the rituals, but so far as I know most masons would not claim much more for them than that they serve to bind the group together and give it its sense of identity. Theological speculation and religious apologetics do not flourish among masons, who simply do not wish to integrate their private language into public discourse. Indeed they choose to move the other way.

There have always been some people in Christianity who have been drawn in this direction. One recalls ancient technical terms like initiation, mystery, symbol (for creed, in the sense of password) and the *disciplina arcani*. The impenetrable jargon of strict sectarians can still be met today. But the truth is that the more the religious vocabulary is made private to the group the more its meaning and truth are made nothing but sociological. And Christians cannot welcome this. A proselytizing religion must *go public*, it must enter its language in the public arena, and accept the empirical and the logical risks of doing so, in the case of Christ no less than in the case of God.

Now in arguing that the philosophy of religion can and should concern itself with belief in Christ I am not principally motivated by the suspicion that natural theology is a lost cause and it would be prudent to move on to dig more fertile ground. What I am saying is that if we are to give an adequate account of belief in God we cannot remain within merely abstract or general rational theism, which barely exists as a *religion*. In Christianity, for example, we can easily demonstrate from liturgical texts that the Christian believer always addresses God through Christ. Whether expressly, or by implication, God is always identified as the Father of Jesus Christ, known "through" him. It is dangerous to analyse Christianity into two elements, theism and the superadded element supplied by Christ.

96

It is not theism *plus* Christ that we meet, in a way which suggests that the two elements could be distinguished and separated, but a form of theism determined and made concrete by Christ, that is, Christian theism. I suppose that it would be similarly misleading to break up the unity of Islamic theism into theism *plus* the revelation through Muhammed in the Qu'ran. It is for this reason that many Christian theologians maintain that the doctrine of Christ completes the doctrine of God, and solves the various problems we have discussed in Part One.

So that if you are willing to permit the application of a philosophical method of enquiry to belief in God, it will inevitably come to be applied also to Christ, as it struggles to come to grips with the actuality of theistic belief.

For the central problem of belief in God is the problem of analogy. Men have an obstinate habit of trying to speak of God in human terms, they *must* so try to speak, and yet apparently they can find no fully satisfactory way of justifying it. How *can* you speak of what is *ex hypothesi* transcendent and can never come to clear expression in human language?

In Christianity it is claimed that God has expressed himself in human form. A man who is in some sense the expression of God in human form has died and is vindicated. Plainly this must have a bearing on the logical problem of how the expression of God in human language can be vindicated. The way dogmatic theology relates the crucifixion and the resurrection to each other is intimately linked with the way in the philosophy of religion we try to relate the impossibility and yet the practical necessity of speaking of God in human language.

But what of the question of the uniqueness of Christ, which is supposed to make Christology peculiarly resistant to philosophical understanding? The popular phrase "the scandal of particularity" is often invoked at this point. Its origin is obscure: perhaps it comes from Germany early in the present century. In England it has been a *cliché* for over thirty years: and as with many phrases which have been much used, it has been used in various senses. I suspect that it probably embraces at least three distinct theses.

Of these, the first is the appeal to paradox or to mystery, probably first introduced into theology by the Cappadocian writers Gregory of Nyssa, Gregory of Nazianzus and Basil of Caesarea in the fourth century. They used it to rebuke the presumption of certain philosophically-minded heretics such as Aetius, Eunomius and Eudoxus: the so-called "Anomoean" party. God, said Gregory of Nazianzus for the first time in the history of Christian thought, is infinite and so can never be perfectly comprehended by a finite intellect.[1] Still less then can we hope to understand the manner of his union with mankind in the Incarnation.[2] The scandal lies in this unthinkability.

The dispute between Eunomius and the Cappadocians has since been repeated many times in theological controversy. Other theses have entered the argument.

For example, it may be argued, in the Thomist manner, that sense bears upon the particular, and intellect upon the universal. Reason grasps a thing by catching it in a net of universal concepts, but what makes it uniquely itself is elusive and must remain so. The individuality of real entities which are not sensible is more elusive, and the union of God and man in Christ, being necessarily unique, cannot in its inwardness be brought under general notions at all. The notion of being human is general, of course, but the notion of being the one person in whom divine and human natures are hypostatically united is not. It can be spoken of by negation; it can be indicated in that we can point to the one of whom it is asserted. But that is all. It cannot be included in any class or placed at the head of a continuous series of degrees of divine presence in human life.

[1] In his *Theological Orations*, especially the second.
[2] Gregory of Nyssa, *Address on Religious Instruction*, II. See also his short treatise, *On Not Three Gods*, for his views on the divine nature.

The third thesis which may be brought forward in this connection has to do with the old philosophical disparagement of historical knowledge, which was particularly strong between Descartes and Kant. Philosophers thought that the term "knowledge" ought to be restricted to cases where the object known is immediately present to the knower, either by way of rational intuition or sense-observation. Historical science could never attain to any higher status than probable belief. Its object is never immediately present to the mind. It is attained only by fallible inferences from imperfect evidence. The scandal then is that our eternal salvation is inextricably bound up with matters of contingent fact of which our knowledge can never be more than merely probable. Lessing confessed himself baffled at this point;[1] Kant more explicitly declares that the object of saving faith cannot be the Jesus of history, but is rather the *a priori* ideal of perfect goodness immanent in our reason, to which so far as we can judge Jesus conformed.[2]

The three theses embraced by the phrase "the scandal of particularity" are then that the union of an *infinite* with a finite nature must be unthinkable; that as a unique event it cannot be understood through general notions; and that our access to the fact of it involves us in the relativities of historical knowledge.

Well, the status of historical knowledge is itself a philosophical question which we must discuss; and I do not see that the other considerations which are grouped under the slogan, "the scandal of particularity" need frighten us off. Indeed we ought to insist that appeal to the unthinkability of the Incarnation and the uniqueness of Christ can be made a pretext for a kind of deception.

For example, it is very important in Christianity that when the first disciples experienced the risen Lord they

[1] *On the Proof of the Spirit and of Power* (1777), in H. Chadwick, *Lessing's Theological Writings* (1956), pp. 51ff.

[2] *Religion within the Limits of Reason Alone* (1793), Book III, Division 1, vii.

recognized Jesus or claimed to have done so. And they insisted that it was the *same* Jesus who had died who was now the risen Christ. Now here we find use made of the concepts of recognition and of continuing personal identity, and there are two possibilities. Either the concepts are applied here in the same sort of way as they are applied in other cases where we recognize somebody and see that he is still the same man, or they are not. If they *are* then the philosopher's accounts of what it is to recognize somebody, and of what it is to be the same man at t_2 as you were at t_1, are profoundly relevant. But if they are not, if the argument is that the recognizing and the identity here in question are unique and incomparable, then we do not know what we are talking about. But in fact the stories, however crudely mythological they are, do in their present form bear witness to the conviction that the risen Lord is still the same Jesus in the everyday sense of *same*. Perhaps he is the same in the sense in which we might say that John Smith after having emerged from some terrible ordeal, and having been scarred and perhaps changed by it, is yet still the same old John Smith: or perhaps we should say that the risen Lord is the same as Jesus in the way that the Prime Minister and Edward Heath are one and the same. There are various concepts of identity. But if we say that the risen Lord is the *same* as Jesus we must be employing one of them, and we must try to say which.

And this is but one instance—albeit a most important one—of a general truth. What is absolutely unique is indeed absolutely unintelligible. We understand by making comparisons, by applying old words to new things. This does not stop us using general terms to speak of particulars. The referring phrase "the capital city of the richest and most powerful nation" is made up entirely of general terms but it designates one entity only and Washington is fortunately unique. Now Jesus was a man who had a genealogy, a culture and a language. In his teaching he may have said new things, but he did not need new words to say them in. We have no evidence that he invented quite new technical terms. Subsequently his followers also used old words in explaining him. The Christological titles which were conferred upon him probably *after* the Resurrection were ancient titles. In fact it was a very long time before any entirely new technical terms were devised in order to explain Jesus. But it would be odd to conclude from this that the early Christians failed to do justice to his uniqueness. Of course they regarded Jesus as unique, and they explained and defended their conviction in the extant vocabulary.

The biblical writings do suggest—as probably all religious documents do—that there is an ineffable, incomparable element in religion. Christ's riches are unsearchable. But there is also an expressible, an articulable element. Comparisons are made, things are said, according to an implicit logic which we can try to make explicit.

There is a feature of religious language which may be called its *vehemence*, and the use of the word *same* in talking of the risen Christ is a good example of it. Another, which we shall discuss, is the vehemence with which people claim to *know* Christ. What I must insist on here is that this vehemence creates a dilemma. It can only be justified if the words *same*, and *know* are really being used plumb in the middle of their ranges of meaning, so that the ordinary criteria for calling somebody the same man are applicable to the risen Lord Jesus Christ, and the ordinary criteria for claiming to know somebody are applicable to the case of knowing Christ.

Unfortunately in religious discourse there is a notorious danger of slipping into slovenly, portentous and inflated idioms. Philosophical questioning can be a valuable corrective. The simple questions *what do you mean?* and *how do you know?* have tremendous power to prune and purge. And if somebody does make a portentous remark about Christ and then refuses to justify it on the ground that the case is unique and it is impious to call for explanations then he is clearly talking nonsense. You cannot both indulge the vehemence and refuse to justify it; or at any rate, if you do, you discredit yourself. So that if someone wants to insist that the risen Lord is none other than Jesus himself his vehement insistence is an invitation to philosophy. His emphatic use of the words *real, true, know, same* makes a claim that what he says is clear, is open to our inspection.

Finally, some definitions. I propose to follow St. Paul's nearly consistent usage and make a distinction between the names "Jesus" and "Christ", associating a distinct kind of predicate with each.

"Jesus" is logically a proper name; the name of a man, a Jew, probably born and certainly bred at Nazareth in Galilee. He lived, very approximately, from 5 B.C. to A.D. 29. During the twenties he was attracted by the eschatological prophet John the Baptist and became an itinerant prophet himself, preaching a rather similar message. He gathered a certain following, and some may have entertained Messianic hopes of him, for it was presumably on political grounds that he was executed by Pontius Pilate, the Procurator of Judaea. That is what we know of Jesus' life with some certainty. We could add something about his teaching. Sometimes I shall refer to him as "the historical Jesus".

The historian's or the historians' Jesus, on the other hand, is the portrait of Jesus presented in a piece or class of pieces of historical writing. An historian's Jesus may be a more or less accurate and objective account of Jesus. In theological debate it is often unclear whether the phrase "the historical Jesus" refers to Jesus or to the historians' Jesus, to the man or to a certain class of portraits, with serious confusion as a result, particularly when theologians argue from the defects of the historians' Jesus to the "irrelevance" of the historical Jesus.

Like the term "God", the term "Christ" is logically not a proper name but a predicable or descriptive term. However, in the Christian belief there is and can be only one Christ, as there is and can be only one God. Thus "Christ", like "God", can be used as a *de facto* proper name. And I shall use the term "Christ" to designate the risen and exalted Lord Jesus worshipped by Christians. Jesus can be talked about by historians, Christ is talked about by theologians: though it is of course part of Christian faith that Christ is personally identical with Jesus.

When I particularly wish to recall that "Christ" was originally a predicable term I shall speak of the Christ, the Messiah, the one who according to Jewish hope would be appointed by God to come and deliver his people. But it needs to be remembered that among the Jews Messianic and other eschatological beliefs have been very various indeed.

After Jesus' death there appeared a sect which held that "Jesus is the Messiah". We cannot be sure whether they held that Jesus had already completed the Messiah's work, or whether they held that Jesus was the Messiah-designate and would soon come to carry out his task. But at least they said "Jesus *is* the Messiah", whether they meant that he had now triumphantly completed his work as Messiah, or that as an afflicted righteous man he had been raised by God after his death to the dignity of the Messianic office. We do not know how far it would be right to say that they worshipped their Christ, but plainly what was distinctive about them was their identification of the Christ with this particular man, as the phrase "Jesus Christ" reminds us. I only assign different meanings to the two terms for the sake of clarity—and it is simpler than the cumbrous expressions "the Jesus of History" and "the Christ of Faith".

There is a third character, variously described as "the Son of God", "the Word of God" and "the Second Person of the Trinity", who according to later belief became incarnate in Jesus at his conception. None of these phrases is very satisfactory, and the first two of them in particular are used in several other senses in the biblical writings. So we may simply call him the Logos, but I shall not discuss him. We shall, in the present discussion, not reach the sublime heights of the developed dogmatic theology. But one group of questions we shall try to answer. Our topic is the structure of belief in Christ; that is, what is it to believe in Christ, and how is that belief related to belief in God? What is the present reference of talk of Christ? An answer to these questions will take us some way to understanding what Christology is all about.

7

A MAN AND HIS MYTH

ON JANUARY 25 each year Scotsmen, whether resident or
expatriate, gather together for Burns Night junketings.
Haggis and wine are consumed and toasts are drunk to
the immortal memory of Robert Burns, to absent friends,
to the lassies and so on. Critics have suggested that these
occasions do not have much to do with the Burns of history.
He did not institute an annual ceremonial feast in his
own memory and would perhaps have been amused by
the myth which sentimental patriots have wrapped about
him. It is true that it is *de rigueur*, in the toast to the immortal
memory, to make some reference (even if a trifle garbled)
to the Burns of history. But the Burns of history as such
is not of any great political import: what matters is the
consolidation of national ties which is done by the idea
of Burns, the Burns of myth. The objectivity of the Burns
of myth, that is, whether or not it is a good portrait of the
historical Burns, is not particularly important, for Scotsmen
gather, not so much to commune with Burns, as through
his myth to celebrate and enjoy their common national
identity. The quest for the historical Burns, scholarly enquiry
into the question of what kind of man Burns actually was,
is irrelevant to the role played by the image of Burns on
Burns Night: indeed it could be positively harmful.

I am not of course in any way poking fun at Scotsmen.
What I am doing is making an allegory of the way some
theologians talk about the Jesus of history and the Christ
of faith, when they are discussing the question of how
important Jesus and historical judgements about him are
to the formulation of Christian belief.

From the point of view of an ardent patriot, one of the snags about Burns is that we know rather too much about the Burns of history. The real man keeps popping up to mock the legend. In another case, such as that of King Arthur, the myth is comparatively unfettered by history. Whereas the referent of the name Robert Burns is a datable particular man who lies in an indicable grave, the referent of the name Arthur is problematic. But for most purposes the referent of the name is an imaginary or fictitious man, the man who bears that name in certain works of imagination. To fix who Mr. Pickwick is we have to cite only one book, but to fix who King Arthur is we have to cite a whole literary tradition, a thousand years in length. In consequence Arthur does not have very definite outlines. Sometimes we see him against a Romano-British backcloth, sometimes in the high Middle Ages. Sometimes he seems to belong to North Wales or Chester, and sometimes to Somerset. Sometimes we see him as a good but weak man whose court is destroyed by faction and his own reluctance to face up to his wife's adultery; sometimes we see him as a tragic hero accursed by an act of unknowing incest; sometimes we see him as a perfect Christian knight. Over the years, Arthur's legend has become too complex for all his characteristics to be compatible in a single man, so that any poet who wants to write a new Arthur-book can consider himself at liberty to make up an imaginary man by selecting a group of compatible characteristics from the tradition, and putting flesh on them. Within limits he is free to make of Arthur what he pleases.

The myth of Arthur has long outgrown the man Arthur, if there ever was a man Arthur. The myth may contain historical elements. Such myths often do, as perhaps the *Iliad* does. But it is hard to be sure where they are. At most the myth may suggest historical hypotheses which in turn suggest lines of archaeological investigation. But it is rather blurring the issues to ask whether there was a real man Arthur. For whatever historical figure triggered off the myth can have had only a very small proportion of all the characteristics which belong to the Arthur of the literary tradition. There may be a man behind the myth but for the sake of clarity it would probably be better to recognize that the Arthur of myth is one sort of entity and the as-yet-unidentified Arthur of history is another: and probably they do not overlap very much.

Now, in what sense does Arthur *live*? It can be said of the myth-Arthur that he still has some imaginative life in him. The literary tradition is still not quite extinct. In modern times there have been fresh contributions to the Arthuriad by R. S. Hawker, Tennyson, Charles Williams, T. H. White, Alfred Duggan and many others. In the world of imagination Arthur has a kind of biography, he still lives and grows. But we must remember that we are speaking metaphorically in saying this. It is a good metaphor, but even the best metaphors are still only metaphors.

One characteristic of the myth-Arthur is that he has a *redivivus* legend attached to him. There is an old story that he is not dead but sleeping in the after-world and that he will return in the hour of England's need.

Such stories of a second coming are very common, and there are a number of them in the Christian tradition. For example there is the belief in the second coming of Elijah, and the question is raised in the New Testament whether Jesus or the Baptist or neither of them is "the Elijah who is to come".

The logic of such language is fairly simple. In the myth, Arthur is the man who saved England in her hour of need. He was a man of destiny. In the time of trouble we found just the man we needed in a way that makes us believe that a good providence will ensure that next time we again have just the same man. Notice that in this realm the office precedes the individual. The hour determines what the man shall be like. The schema "man to save England in her hour of need" was fitted so perfectly by Arthur that when the occasion to fill it arises again the man required will be so like Arthur that he will be indistinguishable from Arthur. He will in effect be Arthur *redivivus*.

Notice, too, that in the myth Arthur sleeps during the interim-time. He is not really alive, he is dormant until his hour comes. The early Christians seem at one time to have tried out a dormant-in-heaven Christology to explain the status of the risen Jesus but to have come to think it unsatisfactory.[1]

In what senses, then, does Arthur "live" in the myth? Well, the myth-Arthur lives only in the sense that people go on reading the books and talking about Arthur. And within the myth one element is the *redivivus* story. But my interpretation of the *redivivus* legend is that it does *not* entail Arthur's continuing personal identity between his first and second comings. To understand it we should consider it in its context, namely certain beliefs in destiny and in historical patterns or cycles. It is the occasion of need, the requirement for a man who has certain characteristics which will "come again", and the expectation of that recurrence is joined with a faith that when the hour comes the man of the hour will be raised up.

Now these analogies of Burns and of Arthur which I am discussing are reminiscent of certain theological opinions about Christ to be met in the pages of Martin Kähler, Paul Tillich, Rudolf Bultmann and others. Here are some of their own words:

> (Kähler) The real Christ, that is, the Christ who has exercised an influence in history, with whom millions have communed in childlike faith . . . is the Christ who is preached . . . the Christ of faith (these words are written in the context of an attack on "the Life of Jesus Movement").[2]
>
> (Paul Tillich, Kähler's pupil) Participation, not historical argument, guarantees the reality of the event upon which

[1] Acts 3: 19–21.
[2] Martin Kähler, *The So-called Historical Jesus and the Biblical Christ* (1892, 2nd edn. 1896): ed. and tr. by Carl E. Braaten (1964), p. 66. Another study of Kähler by Braaten in *The Historical Jesus and the Kerygmatic Christ*, edd. Braaten and R. A. Harrisville (1964), pp. 79–105.

Christianity is based. It guarantees a personal life in which the New Being has conquered the old being. . . . Whatever his name, the New Being was and is actual in this man.[1]

(Bultmann) Faith in the resurrection is really the same thing as faith in the saving efficacy of the cross . . . Christ meets us in the preaching as one crucified and risen. He meets us in the word of preaching and nowhere else. The faith of Easter is just this—faith in the word of preaching.

It would be wrong at this point to raise again the problem of how this preaching arose historically, as though that could vindicate its truth. That would be to tie our faith in the word of God to the results of historical research. The word of preaching confronts us as the word of God. It is not for us to question its credentials.[2]

Jesus has risen in the kerygma . . . Jesus is really present in the kerygma. . . . If that is the case then all speculation concerning the modes of being of the risen Jesus, all the narratives of the empty tomb and all the Easter legends, whatever elements of historical fact they may contain, and as true as they may be in their present form, are of no consequence.[3]

These remarks, and others like them, have led to a great deal of controversy, which has raised more dust than it has shed light. At first glance they sound like expressions of preference for the Burns of Burns Night, or the myth-Arthur, rather than the historical Burns or Arthur. The story is a long one, going back (as we saw in the last chapter) at least to Lessing and Kant. Inevitably they prompt us to ask how far, and in what sense, the truth of theological statements about Christ is dependent upon the truth of historical statements about Jesus of Nazareth?

In our attempt to clarify this question we shall make use of two very simple logical tools. The first is the distinction between meaning and reference, and the second is the distinction between a necessary and a sufficient condition.

Let us consider first the distinction between meaning

[1] Paul Tillich, *Systematic Theology*, Chap. VIII (U.K. edn., Vol. II, p. 131).

[2] *Kerygma and Myth*, ed. H. W. Bartsch, tr. R. H. Fuller (1953), p. 41.

[3] From Bultmann's 1960 paper, repr. in Braaten and Harrisville, p. 42.

and reference. The meaning of a word, as a glance at the dictionary shows, can be defined in many ways. Proper names do not occur in the dictionary because they do not have meaning, but only reference. However, a proper name can gather round itself a set of descriptive phrases, and these can be cited by way of a definition. Indeed we have assigned distinct "meanings" to the names "Jesus" and "Christ" even though (in the Christian belief) they both designate one and the same individual. Some words, like articles and conjunctions, can only be defined by describing the way they are used. Words like "yellow" are defined ostensively by citing a number of things which *are* yellow, and leaving the reader to grasp that it is yellowness which they have in common. Many words are defined by synonymy. Another word or phrase is given which will, in at least some contexts, be substitutable for the word being defined without changing the force of what is said. And so on. Very broadly, one may say that someone knows the meaning of a word when he has got into the way of using it so that the rest of us can grasp the force of what he says.

The word "Christ" originally designated a certain office or role. It is like the term "Prime Minister". The meaning of the word "Christ" can be defined linguistically in a series of theological statements relating him to God and to mankind, just as the term "Prime Minister" can be defined in a series of statements describing his constitutional role and so on. Grasp the meaning, and you know how to use the term.

The referent of a name or a referring phrase is outside language. It is the actual entity designated by the referring phrase or named by the proper name. The phrases "the morning star" and "the evening star" have different meanings, but the same referent, namely the planet Venus. The phrase "the present Prime Minister of Great Britain" keeps the same meaning, but has over the years a succession of different referents.

The present Prime Minister is Edward Heath, so that

if I use the expression "the Prime Minister" in a sentence in the present tense you will very properly take me to be referring to Edward Heath. My statement is *about* him. However there is from time to time an interregnum in the office of Prime Minister. During an interregnum the phrase "the Prime Minister", though it still has meaning, lacks a referent. At ordinary times, there is no doubt that a statement such as "The Prime Minister is now answering questions in the House" has a clear meaning. We know and can state what state of affairs the expression asserts to obtain, we know that it is a state of affairs which *might* obtain, and we know how to verify whether it is in fact the case that he is answering questions in the House. But during the interregnum there *is* no Prime Minister so that statements about what the tenant of that office is doing are out of order.

These considerations, I believe, prove that language is at least sometimes used to talk about things outside language, and therefore that you cannot give a complete account of meaning in abstraction from questions of reference. And I will go on to maintain that the meaning of talk about Christ cannot be fully explained in terms of the use of the word "Christ" in kerygmatic language.

What then do we make of the expressions "Christ meets us in the word of preaching", he is "risen in the kerygma"? Obviously the meaning of the term "Christ" in Christianity is given in the theological assertions made about him in the preaching of the Christian gospel. Presumably if a man can use the term "Christ" accurately he can be said to know its meaning. However, it would certainly seem that some of the assertions made about Christ in Christian preaching are meaningless or at least seriously out of order unless the term Christ has a present living referent. For in Christianity the office of being the Christ is no longer vacant. Someone is asserted, in the kerygma, to have assumed it. And he is spoken of as showing certain attitudes, doing certain things.

Thus when Bultmann asserts that Jesus Christ is really present in the kerygma and nowhere else we must beg him to be a trifle more explicit.

At one level, what he says is a tautology. The theological import of Jesus Christ can only be expressed in theological statements. Non-theological statements such as "Jesus died by crucifixion" do not convey the religious significance of Jesus. What he is in Christianity can only be conveyed in kerygmatic statements such as "Jesus died for our sins". However, Bultmann certainly appears to go beyond this. For he appears to be saying that the referent of the name Jesus Christ can only be given by pointing to occasions of preaching, and given there in a mysterious manner whose logic cannot be made clear. Speculation about the mode of being of the risen Christ is of no consequence, he says. This could mean one of two things. It may be that the name Jesus Christ does have an actual extra-kerygmatic referent, but that the limits of our faculties make it impossible to apprehend it. Or it may be that Jesus Christ is an entity of the same kind as King Arthur. The name King Arthur has perhaps a remote and for most purposes relatively unimportant actual referent, namely the historical Arthur, but in general literary use the term King Arthur names an imaginary entity, the myth-Arthur, who exists only in discourse and in thought.

If you say that the referent of the title "the risen Lord Jesus Christ" can only be indicated by pointing to occasions of kerygmatic utterance, you leave it rather unclear whether in those occasions summed together there is comprised the whole reality of what Jesus Christ is or whether Jesus Christ has a supra-kerygmatic, that is, an extra-linguistic, mode of being. Bultmann wishes to keep this possibility open, but he cannot keep it open in any intelligible sense because he systematically excludes any possibility of stating it clearly. Yet, unless one can indicate its present referent, kerygmatic talk about Jesus Christ has no clear meaning. It is in the same no-man's-land as talk about what the

Prime Minister is doing during an interregnum in that office.

H. H. Price has recently made the following remark about belief in God: "The theist does not merely propose that we make use of the *concept* of a creative and loving Supreme Being. He asserts that this concept has an instance".[1] Similarly the Christian theist must assert that the phrase "risen Lord Jesus Christ" designates a real entity. It is not sufficient simply to point to occasions where it is used, in preaching, to establish its reference convincingly. Bultmann certainly appears to reduce the presence of Jesus Christ in the world to a chain of miraculous linguistic occasions when one preaches and another believes. Hence Professor MacKinnon's use in connection with him of the telling phrase, "theological occasionalism".[2]

The second logical instrument I promised to produce was the distinction between a necessary and a sufficient condition. It has been repeated endlessly that Christianity is established, based, founded, grounded or anchored in history, rather in the manner in which someone might reassure us that a great balloon is safely moored. It is much less common for people who use such metaphors to say in logical terminology what they mean. But I suppose the commonsense view would be that the truth of an historical statement about Jesus of Nazareth is a necessary condition of the truth of any particular theological statement about Jesus Christ. It is of course perfectly possible to believe in Jesus Christ without having the desire or the ability to grapple with questions of historicity. But if you seek to *justify* a theological belief about Jesus Christ, then in the course of your attempt you must introduce an historical statement. Unfortunately in the vast literature on this subject people have often failed to distinguish between the act of believing, which may well be independent of historical

[1] *Belief* (1969), p. 460.
[2] *Borderlands of Theology* (1968), p. 85. The author tells me that the phrase was first used of Karl Barth; but it fits Bultmann better.

research, and the systematic attempt to explain and justify the content believed, which is not.

Suppose one takes a theological statement such as "Jesus died to save us". Then it is a necessary condition of the truth of this statement that as a matter of historical fact there was a man named Jesus who died. Plainly it is not a sufficient condition. We must introduce other and theological premisses in order to make a valid inference from "Jesus died" to "Jesus died to save us". But a historical statement about Jesus, though not a sufficient, is a necessary condition. And so no theological belief about Jesus Christ can escape the fact that one of its premisses involves it in the realm of contingency, of probable inference and human fallibility. Accordingly historical research can falsify a Christological statement, but cannot of itself confirm it.[1]

In the Anglican baptism service there is an exhortation designed to encourage those who bring an infant for baptism. A passage from the Gospel of St. Mark is read, which describes Jesus blessing children. The exhortation then argues that

(i) Jesus was p;
(ii) Jesus is the Christ;
(iii) Jesus Christ is the same yesterday, today and forever; and so it concludes
(iv) "Doubt not therefore, but earnestly believe" that Jesus Christ is now p.

The suggestion here is, I think, that every kerygmatic statement of the form "Jesus Christ is now p" presupposes some historical assertion to the effect that "Jesus was p". At least this is true where the moral attitudes and dispositions of Jesus Christ are in question.

But now we have a puzzle. In the example just quoted "Jesus Christ is p" was proved from one historical and two theological premisses. How shall we in turn prove

[1] See F. G. Downing, *The Church and Jesus* (1968), p. 181.

those theological premises? Presumably they also will each need a historical statement to "anchor" them. Let us try to do it, taking (iii) above first:

  (i) Jesus was morally constant, in his love for sinners, and in his obedience to God's will;
  (ii) Jesus is the Christ, the Christ is none other than Jesus;
  (iii) ∴ Jesus Christ is the same yesterday, today and forever.

Now we have to prove that Jesus is the Christ:

  (i) According to Israelite expectation the Christ should have characteristics a, b, c . . . n;
  (ii) Jesus had these characteristics;
  (iii) ∴ Jesus is the Christ.

Now these arguments which we have constructed are much too crude, and conceal innumerable complexities. But they suggest how some people have come to think that if you work away long enough at theological statements about Jesus Christ you will be able to convert their historical necessary conditions into sufficient conditions, for in the last syllogism the premises are purely historical. There might be an indefinite regress, but at least if the *whole* story were told, faith and fact would match intimately. This I believe may be the position maintained by Dr. Alan Richardson, who runs very close to saying that the Christian beliefs can be proved or made highly probable from historical premises alone.[1] In this opinion he has a certain amount of popular support: but the philosophers are all but unanimous against him. After a careful discussion the late Austin Farrer sums up: "Is Revelation-History just history? Its matter is historical, its interpretative concepts not simply so, for their reference is not to patterns of finite event alone; they refer to a transcendent agency."[2]

So the last of our syllogisms above did not prove that

[1] In his book, *History Sacred and Profane* (1964). See the discussion in J. Navone, *History and Faith in the Thought of Alan Richardson* (1966).
[2] *Faith and Speculation* (1967), p. 173.

Jesus is the Christ from historical premises alone. All it showed was the reasoning by which, given the contemporary belief system, some Jews recognized the Messiah in Jesus. The truth of Jewish beliefs about God and his Messiah is another matter, and an historical explanation of how those beliefs arose is always something different from a demonstration that they are true. Theological statements about Christ cannot be *completely* analysed into historical statements about Jesus and contemporary Jewish beliefs.

If you and I look into the doors of a church at half-past eight on a Sunday morning you may remark to me "There is a service in progress". Or you may say "A priest is celebrating Mass". Or you may say "People are receiving the body and blood of Christ". The first of these remarks may be simply empirical. In the second you are borrowing, perhaps in a non-committal way, the special terminology of the Church. But by the time you make the third remark you are quite plainly employing concepts whose "reference is not to patterns of finite event alone; they refer to a transcendent agency".

So it would appear that Christological statements begin where theological concepts are applied to matters of historical fact. You may go some way to explain how those theological concepts themselves developed historically, but you can never prove that they have reference simply by historical reasoning. Some of the successors of Bultmann at present are in a muddle if they suppose that by showing historically how the preaching of Jesus developed into the preaching about him you can validate the latter. Bultmann is quite correct in pointing out the limitations of what can be achieved by historical argument alone.

At the opposite extreme there stand those who will not allow that the truth of historical statements about Jesus is either a sufficient or even a necessary condition of the truth of theological statements about Jesus Christ. In order to safeguard what they consider to be the certainty of faith (i.e. the certainty that some theological statements about

Jesus Christ are true) they assert that the truth of such statements can be adequately verified in present Christian experience. Given then that certain theological statements about Jesus Christ are known to be true, it is possible to infer their historical presuppositions. The outstandingly interesting case is that of Paul Tillich, and we must analyse it in detail.

How far can a theological statement be verified in experience? Let us take an analogy from Buddhism.

In Buddhism it is claimed that the following of the Noble Eightfold Path leads to Enlightenment. We may imagine a disciple setting out to test this proposition. He follows the path, is encouraged by reading stories of Gautama, and at last himself achieves Enlightenment. He might thus verify the central Buddhist claim in a way logically independent of the historicity of the various items in the body of teaching which has guided him. The itinerary is verified because it works.

Could a Christian similarly verify the Christian way to salvation? If so, it might be claimed, the saviour is in effect the preached Christ of the church. If *he* transforms lives then historicity does not matter, just as if the myth-Arthur inspires poets the historical Arthur does not matter.

The Buddhist might then argue that he must have at least one predecessor along the road from whom the knowledge of the route originates. *Mapped* territory cannot be virgin territory: some one must have been there before him. Notice though that the disciple has only verified the map so far as it has led him, and he has only verified the whole itinerary when he himself has reached his final destination.

Tillich's argument is similar in form.[1] Christian faith is participation in the New Being. This new mode of life upon which the believer enters is received from beyond himself: it cannot have been evolved from within himself

[1] *Systematic Theology*, Chap. XVII (U.K. edn. Vol. II, pp. 112ff.)

and his own resources. Yet it is a human mode of life, enjoyed within an historical community. There must then have been a first man who inaugurated it. But we can say more than that about him, for the New Being has a moral structure, "it is the picture of him in whom it has appeared".[1] So although there may well be uncertainty about details the believer is justified in asserting an *analogia imaginis*, a likeness like the likeness of a true portrait, between the ecclesiastical image of Jesus as the Christ and the man from whom the picture has arisen. However, it is of course the picture which has the transforming power, and not the hypothetical man behind the picture. By this theory Tillich both maintains that Christian faith has an historical foundation and makes that foundation impregnable against the results of historical research.

The idea of a kind of metaphysical deduction of historical statements about Jesus was not new. In some Hegelians it reached dizzy heights. The egregious Daub deduced *a priori* from the idea of God not only Jesus but even Judas Iscariot.[2]

Tillich's argument has already been very extensively discussed and criticized. Notice however that he is in agreement with many theologians upon two propositions. The first is that the proximate object of Christian belief is Christ, the exalted Lord of faith, and that Jesus, the Jesus of history, is at best its remote object. The second is that the latter is accessible only through the former.

Where Tillich's argument is incomplete can be shown by constructing an analogous argument, taking for example the character of Mr. Casaubon in George Eliot's *Middlemarch*.

(i) Mr Casaubon is a very striking and vivid creation.
(ii) Novelists very commonly base at least their best characters on real people.

[1] *Op. cit.*, p. 132.
[2] See O. Pfleiderer, *The Development of Theology* (1890), p.132.

(iii) To make her character of Casaubon really "live" George Eliot will probably not have altered him very much from whoever was her model.

(iv) There was then in all probability a man who was the model for Mr Casaubon, and though we cannot be quite sure which characteristics are shared by Casaubon and his archetype we can safely assert that there will be an *analogia imaginis*, a resemblance between them.

(v) Mark Pattison, an acquaintance of George Eliot, clearly fills the bill.

(vi) There are good independent grounds for thinking that George Eliot did in fact take Mark Pattison as her model.

Now of the six steps in this argument no less than three are missing from Tillich's parallel argument, namely (ii), (v) and (vi). He might try to replace (ii) by claiming that new life-styles are always inaugurated by men who embody them perfectly, but it is hard to see how he could justify this general proposition. What about, for example, Tolstoy? Or he would, more probably, appeal to the uniqueness of the case of the New Being: but this is, as we have argued, merely to admit that his argument is defective.[1]

Is the analogy with verifying a map adequate? In order to verify that the itinerary proposed to me really will conduct me to my destination I must complete the entire journey. We saw that only on reaching Enlightenment was the Buddhist disciple entitled to claim that the itinerary for reaching it must have been first drawn up by someone who had discovered the way before him. Similarly if Christians wish to claim that the saving power of the "Biblical Picture of the Christ" is verifiable in Christian experience they must make very bold claims for that experience if it is to become independent of historical support and even

[1] Cf. the argument that we have no reason to reject the gospel miracles because there has only been one Incarnation, and we do not know *a priori* what an incarnate God may or may not be able to do. But if we have no idea of what course of life is suitable for a god-revealing man to live, how can we judge Jesus to be such a man? Making the case *quite* unique undermines all argument.

able to generate historical affirmations. I have no grounds
for claiming that the salvation God offers me through the
preached Christ is genuine and final until I have experienced
the full reality of salvation.

There thus arises a contrast between two markedly
different sorts of Christian. There is one who believes that
he is on the way to salvation because he believes to be
true certain theological judgements upon the history of
Jesus. And there is another who seems to claim immediate
knowledge of his saviour and possession of all the blessings
of salvation and therefore concludes that his saviour must
have entered the historical realm at some past time. Since
as a matter of fact it is within the Christian tradition that
he has found salvation he thinks it reasonable to identify
as his saviour the enigmatic, little-known man who stands
at the head of that tradition. Thus the identification of
Jesus of Nazareth as his saviour stands not at the beginning
but at the end of his train of reasoning.

And these two different sorts of Christian have different
attitudes to the question of history and faith. The former
begins from Jesus. He says that it is reasonable to hold
that certain events took place, and to some extent you can
explain and show to be reasonable certain theological
generalizations upon those events. And so he believes that
the man in Palestine will prove to be his saviour, and he
sees some confirmation (if not a full verification) of his
belief in his consequent moral experience as a member of
the Christian society. Final verification must wait, but there
is enough "to go on" in the meanwhile.

The other sort of Christian says, I have already found
salvation by entering into a certain way of living as a
member of a certain community. This way of living is
superhuman yet truly human. Behind the historical origin
of the language in which the New Being thinks itself must
stand the mysterious event of the actual inauguration of
the New Being in human life. Though there are uncertainties
about specifying details here they do not matter very much.

For the picture of Jesus as the Christ is vindicated by its present transforming power, not by appeal to past history.

We may quote here Bultmann's saying that "the combination of historical report and kerygmatic christology in the Synoptic Gospels is not for the purpose of giving historical legitimacy to the Christ-kerygma, but quite the reverse, of giving legitimacy to the history of Jesus as messianic history, as it were, by viewing it in the light of the kerygmatic Christology".[1] This sentence is very obscure, but at least it is clear that Bultmann's thought moves from Christ to Jesus rather than the other way round.

Our discussion so far has shown, I think, that the interpretation of Christianity offered by Tillich, Bultmann and others resembles Catholic Modernism. I have suggested already many reasons for doubting whether it is workable. On philosophical grounds it would seem that the sort of Christology which begins from Jesus is more coherent than the sort which begins from present knowledge of the Christ of faith. A final decision on this point, though, must wait until we have formed some opinion of claims to know Christ immediately in religious experience. If those claims cannot be upheld, or are found themselves to presuppose a reference to Jesus if they are to be tenable, then that will clinch the matter.

Ten years ago R. W. Hepburn concluded that "no amount of subtlety can provide historicity without the risks of historicity".[2] It looks as if that verdict still stands, though we have some way to go yet in our argument. But here is a double-edged thought on the matter: the risks of historicity are no worse than metaphysical risk. If religious faith makes any metaphysical claim about the reality of God that claim is liable to refutation by philosophical argument. To admit a historical risk in talk of Christ is no worse than to admit a metaphysical risk in talk of God. If anything in the way

[1] Braaten and Harrisville, pp. 24–5.
[2] *Christianity and Paradox* (1958), p. 110.

of descriptive force or empirical content is to be claimed for religious utterances then some risk must be taken. To make a claim is to lay oneself open to the possibility that it may be refuted.

8

HISTORY AND THEOLOGY

OUR PREVIOUS enquiry left us with the question, is it or is it not the case that the truth of an historical statement about Jesus is a necessary condition of the truth of a Christological statement? At first sight it might seem that one might move the other way, from theology to history, for if the theological statement is true then the historical statement presupposed by it must be true. But how can the truth-value of the theological statement itself be determined, so far as it does contain an historical element, except by use of the historical method, among other things? If every statement about Christ is a statement about one who is none other than Jesus, historical argument must necessarily contribute to establishing the reference of talk about Christ. No one should claim that the historical method alone can validate a Christological statement. But it would seem to play an essential part in establishing *one* of the two main sorts of premiss needed to justify any Christological assertion.

At one extreme some theologians join Dr. Richardson in making Christological statements all history, and at the opposite extreme there are those who would make them all theology. But commonsense would suggest that the literary form of a Gospel clearly shows a blending of the two elements. And the early Christians *argued* in attempting to justify Christological assertions. It is not correct to say that they did not argue, but preached, as if no preaching could be arguing and no arguing could be preaching. On the contrary, they preached arguments.

In these arguments they tried to exhibit the fulfilment of scripture in the career of Jesus. That is to say they tried to demonstrate a certain match or correspondence between certain theological concepts and the facts of Jesus' life and death (e.g. Luke 24, 13–35). The facts were such as to make the application of the concepts appropriate, if you looked at them in the right way. On Bultmann's view, that the Christian preaching presupposes the bare "that" (as he calls it) of Jesus, with no descriptions attached, Jesus is reduced to a bare peg, and the vast apparatus of Christian belief could just as well have been erected upon the person of the Baptist or indeed any other contemporary figure recently deceased, such as Judas. What's in a name if no descriptions are attached to it?

Whatever the origin of the sermons in the book of the Acts of the Apostles, at some stage in the early history of Christianity they must have been regarded as good examples of apologetic method. In these sermons the preachers argue that Jesus is the Christ, or that the Christ has come and his name is Jesus: and clearly such an argument can only be articulated in the form, Jesus had certain characteristics which it is appropriate that the Messiah should have. Empirical predicate of Jesus must be matched in detail against theological predicate of the Messiah.

In some of the sermons the argument goes one way, in some another. It could start from Jesus and appeal to certain known facts about him, and then argue that they match messianic expectation. Or it could start from the messianic expectation, pointing to certain features of it, and then argue that this schema has in fact been fulfilled in Jesus. It could be argued, that is, either that Jesus is the Christ (e.g. Acts 2: 36) or that the Christ is Jesus (e.g. Acts 8: 26–35; 17: 1–3; 18: 28).

These two possible directions in the argument are presumably the basis of Bultmann's distinction between using the appeal to the historical Jesus to legitimate the Christ-kerygma, and using the Christ-kerygma to legitimate the history of Jesus.[1] But his term 'legitimation' is vague, and

[1] Cited above, p. 121.

his distinction unreal. For the logic is the same whichever way the argument goes. Either way, Christological assertion arises when historical fact and theological concept meet, and both are necessary. Bultmann himself acknowledges that the Gospels combine "historical report and kerygmatic Christology", and it is not surprising that his former pupil Ernst Käsemann should challenge him to explain why, on his other views, people should have thought it necessary to write such a book as a Gospel? If the life of Jesus is irrelevant to the kerygma why write a kerygmatic book in the form of a life of Jesus?[1]

As we have said, the present German controversy is somewhat confused by the fact that his critics are pleading for historical continuity between Jesus and the Christ-kerygma, whereas Bultmann (insistent as ever upon the *novelty* of the kerygma) is maintaining that even if you could demonstrate historical continuity (a phrase which he rightly says has various meanings), that demonstration could not justify the kerygma. Bultmann is partly in the right of it here. To show how belief *p* developed into belief *q* is not to show that *q* is true. Historical connections are not logical connections. On the other hand Käsemann is right in saying that the Christian kerygma is after all a theological interpretation of the career of *Jesus* and not of the Baptist or Judas. The writing of a Gospel, whenever it was done, and whoever did it, constituted an appeal to history.

Bultmann's opinions are strongly reminiscent of certain views which have been aired in the British debate upon the philosophy of religion by Wittgenstein and others such as R. M. Hare and T. R. Miles.[2] The suggestion is that a religious concept is in no sense *a posteriori*, or derived from

---

[1] *New Testament Questions of Today* (1969), p. 40f.

[2] L. Wittgenstein, *Lectures and Conversations* (1966), pp. 71f.; R. M. Hare, in *New Essays in Philosophical Theology*, edd. Anthony Flew and Alisdair MacIntyre (1955), pp. 99ff.; T. R. Miles, *Religion and the Scientific Outlook* (1959).

experience: it is *a priori*, and applied to experience. Wittgenstein talks of using a picture, and his successor John Wisdom has talked of religious beliefs as patterning experience.

Such an account of the logic of religious concepts has many difficulties. It has to be explained how the concepts come to be framed in the first place, why it should matter which religious concepts a man adopts, how it is that people come—as they evidently do—to modify their religious views, what is the nature of theological controversy, and how it comes about that religious faith can be put to the test by the way things go, if its logic is such that it is in principle unfalsifiable. And such questions can only be answered by appealing to experience, by showing that experience lends itself to this interpretation rather than that.

Bultmann's view of the kerygma is open to similar objections. He talks as if it fell from heaven ready-made: he believes in the kerygma as a linguistic miracle, though he has freed himself from the notion of physical miracle. But such historical evidence as we have suggests that the kerygma was formulated by men, who argued their way into it. Of course, in so far as a sacred text contains arguments we have to apply logical criteria to evaluate the arguments: it is no longer simply a sacred text. Bultmann, denying argument any serious function in theology, sees his task as simply "reinterpreting" the *conclusions* of the New Testament writers.

If we try to reconstruct the arguments by which men arrived at the beliefs expressed in the kerygma we will find that their premises, and the methods of arguing, are in many ways strange to us. But at least we can say that in the arguments certain current theological ideas are applied to the history of Jesus. So that there *is* room for two distinct enterprises: ascertaining the facts about Jesus, and arguing about their theological interpretation.

How then has it come about that a number of modern theologians have been so attracted by idealist philosophies of history?

The answer, in a word, is that both in philosophy and in theology there has been a long-held assumption that there can only be *knowledge*, in the strict sense, of what is immediately present to the mind. Both philosophers and theologians have exalted immediate knowledge and disparaged inferential knowledge.

The theologians thought something like this: faith insists upon the importance of knowing Jesus Christ as one's personal saviour. He must in some way be apprehended as a contemporary, recognized as alive in the Christian man's present religious experience. What Luther called historical faith, that is, mere assent to historical propositions about Jesus, cannot save. The Jesus of history is past, and cannot as such be the object of saving faith. Nevertheless, it is obviously the case that someone who claims to "know" Christ will, if pressed, claim to "know Christ through the New Testament". The New Testament furnishes the concepts by which Christians interpret their present experience, and the tokens of recognition by means of which they identify Christ at work in the contemporary world. Jesus Christ is cognized in the New Testament and on that basis recognized in the hearts of believers. So the New Testament is used as if it were a contemporary book.

It seemed that idealist philosophy could help to explain how this could be done; how, that is, the New Testament could be used as a contemporary book.

And in the philosophy of history at this point there was an unholy alliance of positivists and idealists. For both took it that there can only be *knowledge* in a case where what is known is immediately present to the mind, whether as object of observation or as object of creative rational thought. Both positivists and idealists tried to argue that because historians can only pronounce *upon* the evidence presently available to them, their pronouncements must really be *about* (that is, refer to) the evidence presently available to them. The object of historical knowledge, if it be knowledge, must be present.

Now the positivists liked to hold that the meaning of a statement is given by citing the observation-statements which verify it. So the historian's statements about the past, upon analysis, can be broken down into statements about the contents of the documents presently before his eyes.[1]

And the idealists said, everybody knows that it is by definition impossible to test and therefore meaningless to assert any alleged correspondence between historical statement and historical fact. The historian must rather be seen as contemplating the evidence presently available to him and educing from his own inner resources an imaginative construction which will save the phenomena. History exists only as imagined by historians. Some bold spirits went on to argue that since the objects of historical knowledge exist only *in* present thought, it follows that all history is really the history *of* thought. And since the historian rummages about in his own soul in order to clothe his imagined characters with life-like intentions, it was argued that the purpose of doing history is to gain self-knowledge.[2]

Both the positivist and the idealist were seriously confused in all this. The positivist failed to grasp the logical differences between evidence and conclusion. The idealist failed to distinguish between the thinking of a thing and the thing thought.

Nevertheless it all seemed a godsend to the perplexed Gospel critic. If he was being accused of bringing unacknowledged presuppositions to his interpretation of the Gospels, or of seeing his own face there, or of being unable to establish a body of objective historical statements about

[1] A comment on this opinion in Patrick Gardiner, *The Nature of Historical Explanation* (1952), 1968 edn., p. 39, n. 2. On why such reductive analyses fell from favour, see J. O. Urmson, *Philosophical Analysis* (1956), Chap. X.

[2] Especially R. G. Collingwood, *The Idea of History* (1946).

Jesus it was a great relief to him to learn that he was not to blame, that it could not be otherwise, and even that he was doing the right thing. The idealist philosophy seemed to show that it was right to give up the ideal of objective, scientific, presuppositionless history-writing as unattainable and absurd. The only accessible Christ was the Christ who is *in* the documents, the New Testament picture of the Christ, the Christ meant in the documents rather than the Christ referred to, and he as the reader thinks him, is contemporary with the present-day reader. And it was with some satisfaction that Bultmann read in Collingwood the assertion that "history is for human self-knowledge",[1] though it is only fair to Collingwood to say that there are other strands in his thinking besides the sceptical and the idealistic.

The alleged Jesus of history behind the documents therefore fell into some disrepute. It must be remembered that the phrase "Jesus of history" has itself two different meanings. It could mean Jesus himself, the historical man, but it could also mean Jesus as he appears to the presuppositionless historian, the historians' Jesus. It was felt that the application of the critical methods of "objective" historiography could capture next to nothing of Jesus himself. He was so purely a religious figure that he slips through that particular net. His whole *raison d'être* as a man lay in the realm of theology and faith. Only the kerygma could possibly catch him. Objective history-writing can have nothing or almost nothing to say of him.

So a number of arguments against "the quest of the historical Jesus" have been repeated endlessly. But some of them are very bad, and at this stage of our discussion their badness should be obvious.

For example, it has been argued that since the available "hard" historical information about Jesus is not and can never be *sufficient* to justify the Christian claims about him it is not *necessary* to their justification, so that the attempt

[1] R. Bultmann, *History and Eschatology* (1957), pp. 130ff.

to determine "what really happened" is unnecessary. The commission of this fallacy was made easier by the belief that it was next to impossible to determine "what really happened": theologians then felt called upon to give a theological explanation of why the historical Jesus should, in the providence of God, have been made inaccessible to critical historical investigation. The difficulty was very like one urged by the Deists long ago. Why should God have left us so ill-informed? The likely theological answer seemed to be, because we do not need this sort of information, it is not necessary to our salvation. And the theologians drew encouragement from the idealist—or perhaps, relativist— doctrine that presuppositionless history-writing was an idle dream anyway. So it might be argued that the historical Jesus was irrelevant to Christian belief. The fallacy lies in the slide from "insufficient" to "irrelevant".

There is a related argument, which runs as follows: because all hitherto-written lives of Jesus are demonstrably unsatisfactory no satisfactory life can be written. This piece of inductive argument is a clear *non sequitur*. Bultmann's little book about Jesus is by general consent much better than Renan's, and that is what matters. In the pages of every life of Cromwell ever written you can, no doubt, hear an axe being ground: but it is still reasonable to hold that some lives of Cromwell are better than others, and to think that a better book than the existing books may yet be written.

One even hears it argued that since the subjectivity of the historian manifestly enters into all his work all historical writing is biased and none is objectively better than any other. But it would be ridiculous to apply this maxim and conclude that Isaac Deutscher's portrait of Trotsky is no truer than that in the *Soviet Encyclopaedia*.

Another *non sequitur* is this: since we have not the evidence to write a chronologically-ordered biography of Jesus or to make psychological judgements about him we therefore know nothing of importance about him. It does not follow, and indeed there must be very few pre-nineteenth century biographies which are satisfactory in these respects.

A more curious and complex assertion is this: we only know Jesus through the eyes of his followers; we know next to nothing of what he was in himself and how he thought of himself. There is a subtly misleading distinction here between the real man, the inner solitary man, and the man in his social relations, his public image. It is odd to make the "real" man a kind of unattainable thing-in-itself. Surely a man's life just *is* his dealings with others?

Theologians differ about the importance of historical knowledge of how Jesus thought of himself and his mission. Some would say, very plausibly, that it is anachronistic to try to apply modern concepts of self-awareness to ancient material. Some would say that in the case of Jesus, because of the limitations of the available evidence, it happens as a matter of contingent fact to be impossible to say such things as that he went voluntarily to his death with any assurance. Others, like Pannenberg, think the question of Jesus' self-understanding inescapable: that is, they hold that the historian must, with all due caution, express such opinions as he can form. Others regard the entire topic as forbidden ground.

But in general one can say that, in order to make subsequent recognition of the same Jesus by believers possible, all that is necessary is reliable reports as to what it was like to encounter him and acknowledge in him the saving power of God.

This point needs fuller statement. Suppose that there are available in the gospels adequate accounts, built around an historical nucleus, of what it was like for a contemporary of Jesus to experience, in meeting him, the saving presence and power of God. Such accounts have reached us in a form already highly interpreted in terms of later Christological beliefs. But provided that their nucleus is historical, then with their help the later believer may be enabled to discern a certain structure in his experience and so may claim to recognize his saviour as Jesus.

The most highly developed case here is that of a full conversion. It is a commonplace that the man who is undergoing such an experience structures it, interprets it to himself even in the moment of rapture, by means of the religious concepts already available to him. How then can he justifiably claim to have recognized Jesus, a particular man, as his saviour in his experience of conversion? Only if the concepts which he applies to his experience are ultimately *a posteriori*. He can say to himself, to put it crudely, "I have good grounds for thinking that the experience of meeting the historical Jesus and being saved by him from evil had such and such a structure for those people who met the Lord in the flesh. I now experience the same thing. So I can claim that the one who saves me now is the same Lord, who still lives and who still wields the power of God unto salvation."

Thus *if* there is such a thing as an immediate encounter with Jesus Christ in Christian experience[1] *in order to have objectivity it must presuppose reliable historical information about Jesus*. And you cannot use the Christian's experience of Christ to certify what it plainly presupposes without circularity.

Christian beliefs about Christ, then, do presuppose historical statements about Jesus. That is, a certain minimum of reasonably assured historical information about Jesus is a necessary condition of the truth of Christian belief about him and the authenticity of alleged Christian experience of him.

However, it is a distinct question whether Christianity has in fact a sufficient historical basis. All I have argued is that as a matter of logic it needs one, not that it in fact has one.

But people's judgement about this question of fact may

---

[1] As will be seen below, I am doubtful about how far such a claim can in fact be sustained. My present argument is directed against those who would use our supposed present acquaintance with Christ to make up the deficiencies of our historical knowledge of Jesus.

possibly be clouded by bad arguments. One should, for example, be wary of John Knox's[1] argument that the New Testament puts us directly in touch with the Church, not with Christ. If he had simply remarked that the New Testament is entirely written by Christians, and their writings are occasional—that their purpose in writing was to serve some practical need of the contemporary Church—then this would be unexceptionable. But in their writings the early Christians refer to Jesus Christ. They write about him. What we read certainly reflects the church-situation of the writer, and that interest governs his writing. But he does appeal to history and to witnesses. A retired General may write his memoirs with the object of enhancing his own reputation, but if his 'slanting' of the evidence passes a certain point it will begin to be counter-productive. If the New Testament writings are governed by the Church's interest, the Church's interest in turn was to bear true witness to Jesus as the Christ.[2]

So the kind of theology which has sought to make Christian faith independent of the vagaries of historical scholarship is in a cleft stick. If it is hoped to justify Christological beliefs by appeal to present experience alone very bold claims must be made for that experience. And what is more, claims to recognize Christ in present experience, if they are to be justified, themselves presuppose historical knowledge of Jesus. Thus the kind of theology which most needs to make such claims is least able to justify them!

And it is in the same uncomfortable position over the Resurrection. There are two main views about the resurrection, which may be called the *Event* theory and the *Theological* theory. For the present we may define them as follows: on both views it is held that Jesus is risen from the dead, but the historical grounding differs. For the Event

---

[1] *The Church and the Reality of Christ* (1962), p. 22.

[2] F. G. Downing has pointed out that the historical primitive church is, if anything, still more elusive than the historical Jesus: *The Church and Jesus* (1968), chapter I.

theory the belief that Jesus is risen presupposes historical statements about the empty tomb and bodily appearances of the risen Jesus to his disciples. For the Theological theory belief that Jesus is risen appears as a theological judgement upon the course of his life and the manner of his death. But in that case it clearly relies even more than the Event theory upon knowledge of the historical Jesus. It is, I suppose, conceivable that we might have good evidence for an event-resurrection without much knowledge of the life preceding it. But the life which has gone before *is* the evidence for a theological resurrection. So it is very awkward both to be sceptical about historicity *and* to hold a theological theory of the resurrection. You are asserting the conclusion while denying one of its premisses.

However, it is of course possible to be right in holding a belief, without being in a position to justify it. It may be held that Christianity—that is, the Christian belief that Jesus is risen as Lord and Christ and may be known by believers—has a sufficient historical basis, but that basis is inaccessible to us now, after all this time. All we can do is to trust the judgement of those who were in a position to judge, namely the Apostles. We have to believe their belief. The Apostolic faith of later Christians is not so much a sharing in the faith of the Apostles as a faith in them and their trustworthiness.

Thus if a present-day Christian claims to know Jesus Christ, he may be right, but he is not in a position fully to justify his claim. He does not know that he knows Christ, he believes that he knows Christ, and in that belief he rests upon the authority of the Apostles.

Now within such a position various degrees are possible. Suppose you give me ten coins. I look at them. They may be gold, they may be brass, I cannot tell which. You tell me that they are all gold, and I express myself suitably grateful. Now let us distinguish three possibilities.

The first is that I remain simply believing the coins to be gold, but without any way of testing the proposition, or perhaps thinking it would be wrong to put your honesty to the test. In this case I do not *know* the coins to be gold. I merely believe it, perhaps rightly, inasmuch as I believe *you*.

The second is that after applying such tests as I can think of I conclude that in all probability some of the coins are indeed gold and some are brass, but I cannot specify with any certainty which are which. So I decide to keep the whole collection together rather than risk discarding one of the gold ones by mistake.

The third is that after applying tests I am able to conclude with high probability that certain specified coins are brass and others gold.

The allegory is faulty if it suggests that such historical information as the gospels contain is as gold and the didactic and theological revision of it is as mere brass, but let that pass for a moment.

Now, on all three suppositions there are some gold coins, but the epistemological status of my belief that there are differs. In the first case I simply believe you, without any external test. In the second case I am to some extent able to apply a test. In the third case I am able to specify which coins are gold. Your initial assurance suggested to me that it was worth while carrying out the test, but after the testing is done my belief that some of the coins are gold is independent of your authority.

Similarly it may be that Christianity has an adequate historical basis, but that basis is irrecoverable. Christians simply accept without evidence the Apostles' claim that they have adequate grounds for their kerygmatic assertions. Or it may be that we can with more or less accuracy recover the historical basis and retrace the Apostles' reasoning. If so the role of their authoritative proclamation is simply to interest us in examining their case and attending to their arguments.

There is a difference here between the Liberal and the Modernist. The Liberal picked and chose. He reckoned he could extract the historical gold and discard the apostolic theologizing, replacing it with his own theologizing. The Modernist, at once more sceptical and more dogmatic in temper, decided not to pick and choose, but to hold his nose and swallow the lot. The various elements, historical, mythical and didactic are so fused together that there was no chance of being able to separate them.

The Modernist believed that we were in the first of my three possible positions, and the Liberal that we were in the third. But the consensus of opinion among those best qualified to judge suggests rather that we are in the second. Precarious though the whole business is, during the present century there has been considerable progress in reconstructing the early development of Christianity, particularly by form-critical analysis. Altogether this has been a remarkable achievement. In terms of our analogy some tests are available for distinguishing the gold from the brass. That is, it is possible to say with some confidence something of what Jesus was like and to reconstruct the successive stages of thought about him as Christian belief spread from Palestinian Jews to Hellenized diaspora Jews and thence to Gentiles. This reconstruction is already having a great effect upon contemporary Christological thinking and will in the future have more.[1]

In conclusion, there are two elements, both necessary, in talk of Christ: the historical and theological. And they are distinct. There is no judgement about Christ which does not make some historical claim, but equally there is no purely historical judgement which entails a theological judgement. This is consonant with what we have said of God. If he is necessarily hidden or elusive, there can be no quite adequate image of him, and no occurrence in which he is unmistakably displayed.

But it is claimed that there is one great exception. In

[1] See, for example, R. H. Fuller, *Foundations of New Testament Christology* (1965); John Knox, *The Humanity and Divinity of Christ* (1967).

the resurrection, it is said, the realms of theology and of fact intersect, and a statement can be made which is both simply historical and simply theological. I shall deny this claim.

9

GHOSTS, VISIONS AND MIRACLES

WHAT IS meant by talk of the resurrection of Jesus Christ? What really happened? One reply is that we do not know, and cannot be sure because the evidence available is fragmentary, rather incoherent, derives from a remote period and itself dates from some decades after the event attested. There is much to be said for this reply to the *historical* question about the resurrection.

In this morning's newspaper (August, 7 1969) there is a detailed account of a UFO[1] sighting which took place yesterday. I do not take it too seriously. It seems very unlikely that my world-view, my way of living will be seriously affected by these reports. Odd events of this kind are often reported: the Angels of Mons, Russian soldiers marching south through England with snow on their boots, the Loch Ness Monster and the Yeti, ghosts, parapsychological phenomena, and so forth. If the resurrection, and other miracles, are events which belong logically in this company they come up against a good deal of competition for our attention.

The main reason for thinking the resurrection important in spite of all this is that the belief in it is the nucleus of Christianity. I think theologians would be agreed that Christian faith does not merely include as one item among others the belief that Jesus is alive, but is wholly constituted by the fact that he lives. Thus the centrality of the resurrection to Christian belief makes it important to consider it. The central issue of Christology is the relation of fact to faith, and the historical problem of the resurrection is the

[1] Unidentified flying object.

crucial instance of it. And if the resurrection-belief is the nucleus of Christianity, then clearly theologians must give some account of it in order to be able to draw inferences from it and connect it up with other beliefs. And the kind of account a theologian gives of the resurrection will affect much of the rest of his theology.

And in giving such an account of the resurrection the theologian must find himself involved with all manner of philosophical issues. There are the issues raised by the notion of miracle in general—the relation of God to the world, the status of physical law, belief upon the evidence of witnesses and so on. And there are the issues raised by this particular miracle—the relation of personal identity to bodily continuity, what it is to recognize someone, our beliefs about immortality and so on.

If it were quite clear what kind of an event the resurrection is supposed to be, and if the evidence for its occurrence were perfectly consistent and overwhelmingly strong, then we would perhaps have no problem. We could join those who say that the resurrection is the "best-attested fact in history". For them there is no great problem of meaning, and the weight of evidence settles the question of truth. But I think we can safely assert that those who have studied the available evidence most closely are most conscious that there is a problem of meaning. And until the question of meaning is clarified the question of truth cannot be framed correctly.

Thus the theologians' first task is to assign a meaning to the resurrection-belief. This is in the first place a simple problem of exegesis. The available evidence—to be found entirely in the New Testament—is collected, and evaluated. It is, roughly, arranged in order of antiquity and an attempt is made to reconstruct the development of the tradition. In effect this means making a beginning with the passage in 1 Corinthians 15, written in the mid-fifties, in which Paul reminds his readers of the tradition which he had taught them on his earlier visit to them. This tradition he in turn had himself been taught, and indeed he quotes it in language which even at so early a date has already become very formalized.

From this passage enquiry can radiate out in a number of directions. Its literary form can be analysed for traces of its own history. The way it bears upon Paul's subsequent discussion of the general resurrection of the dead can be studied. We can turn to other passages in which Paul speaks of the appearance to himself, such as Galatians 1, and to some extent (but not much) to the accounts in the Acts of the Apostles. Since Peter stands at the head of Paul's list we can turn to other ancient traditions relating to the appearance to Peter, such as the acclamation in Luke 24: 34. Since Paul is the only clearly identifiable early Christian writer of whose thought we know a great deal we can speculate with some profit upon what precisely he took the resurrection to be. And finally we can study the terminology in which the resurrection is spoken of, and in particular the words which are usually translated as "risen", "appeared" and "seen".

One conclusion I would draw at this stage is that so far as we can tell formalized theological confessions of the resurrection faith, seemingly connected with the authorization of apostles, are very much older than the colourful narratives of appearances to individuals found at the end of the Gospels. "The Easter message is . . . earlier than the Easter stories."[1]

In this way a good deal of material evidence bearing upon the historical problem of the resurrection can be gathered. But it is still necessary to frame an hypothesis to account for it. Some will be content to say, here we have a body of evidence that something happened and there is no good reason at all to doubt the good faith of the witnesses, and therefore we may reasonably judge that it did happen. But to argue thus is to beg the question of meaning. What precisely is it that we are judging to have happened? It is

[1] G. Bornkamm, *Jesus of Nazareth* (Eng. trans., 2nd edn. 1963), pp. 182f.

not enough to say "X happened". You have to specify the meaning of X. And here it becomes very difficult to give a clear account. The evidence available to us is itself none too coherent. Was seeing the risen Lord like seeing Edward Heath, or like seeing God, or like seeing the validity of an inference? Was it a physical seeing, a visionary seeing, or an intellectual seeing? Here evidently we are involved with philosophical questions. Or again, consider this argument: The early Christians were insistent that it was none other than Jesus himself, the entire and identical man, whom they recognized in the risen Lord. But our criteria for continuing personal identity necessarily include bodily continuity. Therefore the truth of the resurrection-belief entails the truth of the empty-tomb tradition. Here obviously the attempt to produce a theological theory compatible with the available historical evidence involves philosophical issues.

The question of meaning is also forced upon us when we consider other resurrection beliefs. In many rooms in Cambridge you can see posters bearing the words *Che lives*. Since by the ordinary criteria Che Guevara is dead the acclamation *Che lives*! seems to be formally similar to *Jesus lives*!

There are other moden examples. The American Black Muslims, who originated in about 1918 in Detroit, Michigan, came to believe that their first leader was not merely a prophet but Allah, and exaltation-language gathered about the circumstances of his disappearance. Again, just before King Carol of Rumania submitted to Hitler in 1940 there was a fascist movement in Bucharest called the Iron Guard.[1] They were a rather bedraggled crew of drop-outs and unemployed, and they were jokingly called "the legion of ghosts" because their leaders were all dead men. Codreanu, their *Capitanul* who had been shot two years before, and his associates were believed to be still alive and leading the movement. Their names appeared on its literature.

[1] Described by Olivia Manning in her Balkan Trilogy of novels.

These examples, by the way, expose the weakness of the Beaten-Men Argument which is used almost universally by preachers and writers on the Resurrection. How, they say, could a world-conquering faith have begun among defeated hopeless men unless the Resurrection-faith were true? To which any sociologist could reply, it is precisely among the powerless that such beliefs begin. The Prime Minister does not need a poster saying *Che lives* to encourage him, so he does not put one up.

Of course the use of the term "lives" is highly analogical, and men may even be said to live on after their deaths in a variety of senses. A man lives on in his posterity, an artist or writer in his productions. The spirit of a great national leader may be said to live on and inspire successive generations. It may be said of a man that his name, his memory, his influence, his ideas, things he stood for still live on, though he is dead. In Ulster, says the newspaper, James II is not dead (*The Times*, August 18, 1969).

And again, the resurrection of Jesus, the assertion that he lives, needs to be placed in relation to these other idioms.

What we shall now do is distinguish three families of theories of the resurrection. There are in the first place *Event theories*, which were mentioned in the last chapter. These assimilate the logic of "seeing the Risen Lord" to that of "seeing Edward Heath", with the same kind of objectivity and publicity. Eating and drinking with him, even touching him, were like other acts of eating, drinking and touching. Admittedly no one saw the rising but the meetings with the risen Lord are historical facts just as much as Paul's meeting Peter in Jerusalem.

The strength of theories of this sort is that they do fullest justice to the recognition of the risen and living Jesus, supposing it to have taken place upon the same criteria as we use in other acts of recognition. We recognize by physical tokens. How else can a person be reliably recognized?

What is more, the Event theory is overwhelmingly the plain man's theory. For him, to believe in the resurrection

142

is to believe the Event theory of it. I suspect Professor Lampe[1] found that not one in ten of an intelligent non-theological audience can be persuaded that any other theory of the resurrection is possible. Theologians increasingly tend to find the Event theory incoherent and to look for more plausible accounts. Non-theologians remain obstinately persuaded that whether it be true or false only the Event theory is possible.

Secondly, we have also mentioned *Theological theories*. These maintain that the resurrection-confession was grasped in a flash, as it were, as the Apostles put the facts of Jesus' life and death as they had experienced them side-by-side with the Old Testament. In a shocking flash of recognition everything fell into place and they saw the meaning of this man. The meaning of the belief and the reason for believing were established by a process of argument. Perhaps the conclusion had the force of a revelation when it was first drawn, and could only be described in the language of vision. But basically the resurrection-belief was arrived at by ratiocination. The key theological concept here is that of the fulfilment of scripture—as in the texts (1 Cor. 15: 3b, 4b). The key philosophical concepts can be found in Wittgenstein's analysis of seeing and seeing-as in Book III, Section xi of the *Philosophical Investigations*, a crucial text for all discussion about the relation of fact to interpretation.[2]

Finally, somewhere in between pure Event theories and pure Theological theories are those which arise when we say to ourselves, "Seeing the Risen Lord cannot simply have been an ordinary case of sense-observation because the way he is talked of is different from ordinary talk about a man's appearance and disappearance. The risen body can, apparently, appear and vanish abruptly, be visible to some

[1] See G. W. H. Lampe and D. M. MacKinnon, *The Resurrection* (1966).

[2] A simple presentation of a theological theory in James McLeman, *The Birth of the Christian Faith* (1962). But my version of it is peculiar, and I hope better than that current in Bultmann's school.

and not to others. It seems to be a transformed body, like an ordinary physical object in some ways, but unlike it in others. It would be better to think of a para-normal kind of seeing, a para-normal kind of body. Perhaps we are dealing here with something like seeing a vision". When we think along these lines we are moving into the same kind of realm as that in which people report seeing a ghost, seeing a vision, seeing a UFO, and other odd, out-of-the-body experiences: cases where the thing seen or the manner of seeing it is of such compelling strangeness that it seems to relate us to another world. I shall call this family of theories of the resurrection *Psi-theories*:[1] or if you do not like the name we could call them Vision theories. What I mean are theories which postulate a para-normal seeing of a para-normal object which, it is commonly claimed, is nevertheless available to historical investigation.

Now the resurrection, whatever it is, is something rather odd, so that there is some reason for comparing it with other odd events. There are other cases where people have reported phantasms of the dying, and even, much less commonly, of the dead. Archdeacon Michael Perry, in a neglected book called *The Easter Enigma*, had the courage to gather the evidence of such phantasms, both individual and collective, and to discuss the difficult problem of testing whether they are veridical, in the hope of throwing light upon the resurrection. Since he wrote, Mr. Geoffrey Gorer, in *Death, Grief and Mourning in Contemporary Britain* has gathered evidence—admittedly on a rather moderate statistical basis—that a certain proportion of bereaved persons report both intellectual and sensible visions of the dead, from which they gain comfort.

As well as these parallels there are very remarkable formal parallels between the response to the resurrection-belief and the response to other claims to have enjoyed

[1] Parapsychology and psychical research use the term *psi* to designate the alleged supernatural modes of cognition (such as telepathy) which they study.

some kind of odd experience. There is a logical analogy between the patterns of argument in the various cases; and there is a sociological analogy in that those attracted by the phenomena fall into analogous classes in the various cases.

Taking the logical analogy first, in each case it will be found that the explanations offered by commentators fall into one of five classes:

(i) The first is simple *fraud*. The disciples stole the body (Matthew 28: 13). Spiritualist mediums are often shown to be fraudulent, as in H. G. Wells' novel *Love and Mr. Lewisham*. People are eager for publicity. At least some flying-saucer photographs are fakes. H. S. Reimarus offered an explanation of the resurrection along these lines.

(ii) The second explanation argues that *natural phenomena have been misinterpreted*. H. Paulus suggested that Jesus did not really die, but swooned and subsequently revived.[1] UFO sightings are "floaters" on the eyeball, meteorological balloons, streetlights, celestial bodies, terrestrial aircraft, headlamps on clouds, man-made artificial satellites, the aurora borealis and so on. The Loch Ness monster is a piece of driftwood, a family of otters looping along in single file, a motor boat, vegetable matter raised momentarily by methane bubbles, or a seal that has slipped up the Caledonian Canal from the sea. The Yeti is the Giant Panda.

(iii) The third explanation adduces *suggestibility or psychological disturbance in the experients*. The "subjective vision" theory of the resurrection propounded by D. F. Strauss and many since belongs here.[2] People are prone to imagine things, especially in conditions of stress. It seems reasonable to psychologize when we learn that adolescent girls hear poltergeists, the widowed go to séances, and men in uniform see odd things in the sky.

(iv) The fourth explanation is often said to have been reluctantly adopted in cases where the first three have been

---

[1] So did George Moore, in *The Brook Kerith*; and D. H. Lawrence, in *The Man Who Died*.

[2] Compare the close of Chapter 26 of E. Renan's *Life of Jesus*.

tried and found wanting. It is that *the reports are authentic*; that is, their status is what the sighter takes it to be. So much evidence from reasonable and sincere men cannot be gainsaid.

(v) The fifth kind of explanation is more sophisticated. I will call it the *religious*, using that term in a wide sense. It suggests that many, perhaps most, people have bits of "wild" experience from time to time. They lie behind mysticism, ecstasy, trance, second sight and out-of-the-body experiences. We crystallize and interpret to ourselves such an experience with the help of concepts drawn from our own stock, our culture and life-situation, and so profit from it, making it tell us something to our advantage. The widowed person makes of it a communication from a lost spouse. Fifty years ago people were anxious about life after death in the face of arrogant materialism. So they saw spirits. But nowadays the other worlds that move the imagination are not beyond death but across the sky. People see UFOs instead of ghosts, and they read science fiction instead of ghost stories.

Now if you estimate such wild experiences highly, and believe that one could be veridical and informative given the right interpretative frame, you may entertain an objective-vision hypothesis of the resurrection. At least this suggests an empirical setting for the "telegram-from-heaven" theory first formulated by Keim a century ago in his *History of Jesus of Nazareth* (1867–72).

Odd phenomena or odd claims are then commonly met by one of five explanatory theories which are strikingly analogous whether the subject be visions of the dead, ghosts, or the Loch Ness Monster. The resurrection is often placed in this kind of context and argued about along similar lines.

One obvious objection to the use of any theory of this kind in order to explain the resurrection is the fact that the early Christians repudiated it. In the development of the Gospel tradition we find increasing stress on the physical reality of the appearances. Whatever we make of this, its original purpose was controversial: it was a polemic against those who suggested that seeing the risen Lord was like seeing a ghost. At least the stories show first-century Christians saying that that was *not* what they meant (Luke 24: 37–39). On the Event theory the physical realism in the stories means that Jesus was bodily raised, and bodily seen. He was wholly raised, not a ghost but the man entire. On the Theological theory the meaning of the physical realism is that the one who is called Lord, who is saviour, who is called living, is Jesus in his full historical reality, the whole man and not just his "spirit".

The second analogy between the resurrection and other odd phenomena is sociological. Both spiritualism and flying saucers have generated religious movements. There is the Spiritualist Church and, as an example of an established flying saucer religion, the Aetherius Society. Within these movements functionaries emerge who are analogous to those in other religions. There are the Apostles, the rather miscellaneous group of people who enjoy the initial sightings. There are believers, people strongly attracted by their testimony and willing, for example, to spend the night sitting on a hilltop with bizarre recording instruments looking out for flying saucers, like millenarian Christians awaiting the second coming. There are theologians, who collect evidence, organize apologetics and edit journals. And there are prophets or mediums, who in the Aetherius Society transmit messages from the extra-terrestrial intelligences.

Can the resurrection be thought to belong in this context? Can the claim which it makes upon our interest and attention be compared with the claim made upon us by someone's testimony that he has seen a ghost, a flying saucer, or the Loch Ness Monster? Can the resurrection belief be handled theologically upon the hypothesis that it refers to a psi-event apprehended in a psi-mode of cognition? Is it possible to establish the occurrence of such an event by rational argument, and then to draw theological inferences from it?

To ask this is to ask a general question about the appeal to miracle in evidence of a system of religious beliefs. One is, as it were, first argued into believing that an extraordinary event E has occurred, by appeal to ordinary rules of evidence, and then argued into assenting to a belief-system which gives E a context and makes it intelligible.

The general objection to all such apologetic arguments can, I believe, be fairly simply stated. E is proposed for our belief, and whether we shall assent to it is to be determined by applying the ordinary rules of evidence. Unfortunately, at the *first* stage it is not clear what E is and cannot be made clear. E would not *be* extraordinary unless the notion of it were by ordinary standards internally incoherent: but if so ordinary rules of evidence are inapplicable to it. E has to be both odd enough to overturn our world-view and yet fall under rules of evidence which presuppose our ordinary world-view. So, as Hume rightly says, the definition of a miracle is such that we do not see how testimony could establish it. Suppose E to be a ghost-sighting. The notion of a ghost appears to contain some physical and sensible elements—it can be seen, heard or smelt or some combination of these—and also some non-physical elements. It can come through a stone wall. Now I say, "I don't know what E is, it is a nonsense-notion". "Ah," says the apologist, "Now you are being unscientific. Who are you to define the limits of possibility? By definition we are dealing with something extraordinary, and must keep an open mind." But now the apologist has wrecked his own case. He has made the notion of E so enigmatic and elusive that I cannot lay hold of it enough to be able to apply the ordinary rules of evidence to it. The apologist proposes that I assent to the bare occurrence of E, and at the next stage of the argument is going to oblige me to accept certain consequent beliefs. But I do not know how to apply the ordinary rules of evidence to the claim that E has occurred unless I have an ordinary understanding of what E is supposed to be. If E be a miracle, and a miracle is by definition not capable of incorporation into an historical narrative, cannot be given historical causes according to the ordinary practice of historians and so on, then it is an event which a historian cannot handle. Historians must presuppose the laws of nature. So the attempt to establish the occurrence of a miracle purely historically with a view to subsequently building a system of doctrine upon it must fail.

Another way in which there may be an illicit leap in the argument comes out particularly clearly in the case of UFOs. The apologist will insist that we must accept that UFOs exist, that some things have flitted across the sky which cannot be explained away. But to say that some flying objects have *not* been identified falls a good way short of identifying them as emanating from other planets! There are two distinct concepts of a UFO here. There is the so-to-say *negative* concept of a sighting-report which has not yet been explained, and there is the *positive* concept of something in the sky which has come from another planet. By applying the ordinary rules of evidence the apologist may persuade us of the unremarkable proposition that one man has seen something which other men have not accounted for, and then he tells us that we have been persuaded that UFOs exist in the much stronger sense. And the short answer is, we have not.

Applying all this to the question of the resurrection: there is a familiar apologetic strategy by which we are asked to believe, on historical grounds alone and by applying the ordinary rules of historical evidence, that something very extraordinary occurred after the death of Jesus. In the argument the empty tomb often corresponds to the "negative" concept of a UFO. Appeal is also made to the narratives of the appearances of the risen Lord and perhaps also to St. Paul's conversion and the beginning of the Gentile mission. Then in the second stage we are asked to accept the Christian belief-system as giving the facts a context and an explanation. And here too the reply seems inescapable, if you claim that the resurrection is something so extraordinary that it passes human understanding I do not know what it is that you are proposing clearly enough to be able to apply the ordinary rules of historical evidence to the case.

It is of course conceivable that the empty tomb could be established historically, but only because we know what it is for tombs to be empty; it often happens and nothing in particular follows from the mere discovery that a corpse is missing. For there is no valid argument of the form, the tomb is empty, therefore Jesus is risen. If you are proposing the appearances of the risen Lord as extraordinary and miraculous events they fall outside the applicability-range of the ordinary rules of historical evidence. They fall outside it not so much because they are unique (that is a red herring) but because they are incoherent. How can we evaluate historical evidence of the apparition of a dead man? How can I grasp what such an event is, and estimate the likelihood of its occurrence, when the narratives propose to my assent the apparition of one who in some respects was like an ordinary living embodied person and in some respects not? The intention seems to be to include him in the historical order enough to make him historically accessible, but lift him out of it enough to make the next stage of the argument work. And you cannot have both of these.

Thus what we have called a *Psi-theory* of the resurrection is squeezed out. It is excluded as a meaningless compromise, and the remaining alternatives are the Event theory and the Theological theory.

Let us briefly remind ourselves of what we have excluded. We have considered the hypothesis that the risenness of Jesus was a psi-state of affairs, apprehended in a visionary or psi-mode of cognition. The intention was to try to maintain the objectivity of the appearances, to try to give them a footing in the historical order and so make them accessible to historical investigation while at the same time explaining their quality of being from another world, their metaphysical suggestiveness. But alas, the two aims are not compatible. The instinctive suspicion which the plain man and many scientists feel for parapsychology, psychical research, the occult and all the rest of that rather shady world is well justified. It is a world of confusion, and the resurrection-belief cannot be clarified by being set in such a context.

But can the Event theory, which claims that the resurrection of Christ is a plain historical fact, be stated coherently? Did a corpse get up and walk again? Those who take such a view claim to have tradition behind them. "Christ did truly rise again from death, and took again his body, with flesh, bones (suumque corpus cum carne, ossibus), and all things appertaining to the perfection of man's nature, where-with he ascended into heaven" says the fourth Article of Religion of the Anglican Church; and in this strong language it is joined by the official formularies of all the principal Christian bodies. It is true that the phrase "flesh and bones" has in scripture a different meaning from the phrase "flesh and blood"[1] but this scarcely diminishes the vigorous realism of the language.

And there is something to be said for this bold realism. Many philosophers, like Mr. J. R. Bambrough in his course of Stanton Lectures,[2] maintain that religious beliefs are only clearly meaningful in their crudest form. To be sure, they are false in that crude form: but after the theologians have been at them they are so confused that they do not even attain to the dignity of falsehood; they are merely mean-ingless. Theologians sometimes defend the resurrection-belief on the ground that it is compatible with the materialist thesis, that a person's continuing identity is constituted by his bodily continuity. If you are going to take this line it is ruinous to be fainthearted about it. You must say that a resurrection is nothing less than a matter of a grave opening and a corpse standing up again, as in the case of the for-tunate dead man who was lowered into Elisha's sepulchre

[1] As E. C. S. Gibson points out in *The Thirty-Nine Articles* (1898 et plur. all.), pp. 187ff., it signifies kinship.

[2] *Reason, Truth and God* (1969).

(2 Kings 13 : 21). Christ's resurrection is just like that, and Christ's ascension just like the ascension of Elijah.

Now let us make up an argument. The early Christian belief was that Jesus (and the name denotes a man and a man is his body) was buried and yet rose. The same thing that was put into the tomb came out of the tomb revived with a new and godlike life, and appeared before the eyes of many witnesses. Why call eyewitnesses unless they testify to something which was plainly visible? So the Apostles saw Jesus himself with their mortal eyes, as plain as the nose in your face. But they knew that he had died, had really been dead and buried, so they inferred that he must be risen, though no one saw him rise. It was terrifying, for all that apocalyptic talk of the rising of the dead at the end of the world now applied to something. The end of days was upon them.

Now they believed that a man could only rise from the dead by the revival of his corpse. They had no clear notion of a disembodied person. Once they knew it was Jesus, they knew that he was bodily the same. So their subsequent preaching of the resurrection, after the final parting, implied a claim that the body was missing. And if the authorities had wished to falsify the apostolic preaching they could have done so by producing the body. But it was apparently not producible, and the best they could do was to put about a rumour that the body was stolen, itself a kind of indirect confirmation of the empty-tomb tradition.

At first the Apostles knew only of the appearances to themselves. In that sense the appearances-tradition is indeed older. Perhaps the appearances took place in Galilee, though if we are sticking to our guns we have to imagine the risen Jesus walking there. Anyway, the earliest tradition in the gospels explains that those who first found the tomb empty, being mere women whose evidence was not highly valued under Jewish law, were at first disbelieved. Only after a full and settled conviction of the reality of the resurrection had developed was the empty-tomb tradition joined on to it. People believed the women because they had sufficient independent grounds for supposing that the grave must have been vacated. The women's testimony could then be accepted because it corroborated what they already knew. And all this explains why the empty-tomb tradition is reliable, though it appears late.

Thus the apostles regarded the appearances of Jesus as objective physical events. The bodily features of the apparitions in the stories we have are not just projected expressions of the belief that it was indeed Jesus who had been raised. They were the objective grounds upon which he was recognized as being the same man, tangibly present. There is no good ground for scepticism.

How else can the origin of Christianity be explained, how else can beaten men have become heroic Apostles except by the very strongest evidence that Jesus had conquered death? For them such evidence could only be actually seeing Jesus bodily, and recognizing him as the same. In these matters realism must be consistently maintained. Unless Jesus Christ rose bodily from the grave there is no good ground for saying that he is still incarnate now. The incarnation, the resurrection, the perpetual glorified humanity of the ascended Lord, and the reality of our redemption all hang together. The strength and the sting of the gospel is its offensive crude realism.

Thus the truth of our redemption by Christ can only be defended by strictly carrying through an Event theory of the resurrection.

Well, what do we make of this argument?

10

RESURRECTION-EVENT
OR RESURRECTION FAITH?

IN THE last chapter we distinguished three theories or types of theory of the resurrection, which we called Event theories, Psi theories and Theological theories. We considered Psi theories first and argued that though people have often talked about the resurrection in this way such talk is in the end hopelessly incoherent.

This created a dilemma. Theologians must choose between either a strict Event theory or a strict Theological theory. Either the resurrection belief is founded upon eyewitness testimony to a straightforwardly observed event, namely meeting and recognizing Jesus after his death: or it is founded upon theological argument.

So we have outlined a strict Event theory. The grave opened, the corpse revived and the living Jesus walked: and he must walk and keep on walking in order to appear here and there. You may say that nobody actually holds a view of the resurrection as crudely physical as this. But I am arguing that the crudest form of the theory is in many ways the best and has the clearest meaning, for in so far as people in practice qualify it they are quietly evacuating it of meaning, while still claiming for it the merits which rightfully belong to it only in its crudest form. For when the theory is stated in the crudest form the risen Lord is *alive* in the same sense, he is the *same* Jesus, he can be *recognized* just as a few days before. And so the Event theory on its strictest form can very reasonably appropriate to itself commendatory epithets like *objective* and *realistic*. If some tough-minded person says that Richard is the same person as he was a week ago if and only if we can in principle track his bodily movements without a break during that time, then the theologian can cordially agree. Yes, the very same body that was crucified walked the earth again and was translated to heaven where it still is.

So there is much to be said for the Event theory in a strict form. If, conscious of difficulties in it, people progressively introduce qualifications to protect it from being thought absurdly crude and simply false, they blur its meaning and rob it of its original merits. For example, in so far as it is said that Jesus' risen body was "glorified", "transformed" or "freed from certain physical limitations" it can no longer be claimed on behalf of an Event theory of the resurrection that it remains compatible with the assertion of a necessary connection between personal identity and bodily continuity.

Notice how the old problem of harmonizing the gospel stories changes its form according to whether you do or do not suppose bodily continuity to be maintained by the risen Lord *during the period of the resurrection appearances*. If the risen Jesus can appear now in Jerusalem, now in Galilee, now in Emmaus without walking from place to place then the intermissions show that a strict Event theory has been given up, and it is not legitimate to claim its merits in some contexts while trying to avoid its demerits in others.

But the superiority of resurrection doctrines over immortality doctrines is not quite so great as is sometimes claimed, for they cannot maintain bodily continuity all the way.[1] For if we suppose that while my corpse lies in my grave in Cambridge, somewhere in another world a reconstituted, re-embodied me lives, bodily continuity has been abandoned. Even if my grave in Cambridge be supposed empty, my body still cannot be translated to this other world without a break in its spatio-temporal continuity. Unless heaven is in principle open to astronomical observation I cannot

[1] See S. R. Sutherland, 'Immortality and Resurrection' in *Religious Studies*, vol. 3, pp. 377ff (1968).

by any means be translated to it along a continuous track through space and time. But no one seems to claim that it *is* so open.

There may be another world to which Jesus ascended and for which we are destined after death, and in it we may lead bodily lives. If our bodies there are replicas of our present bodies, with a one-one correspondence of new body to old body, that might assist our *recognition* of personal identity. But we would *not* be able to assert that spatio-temporal bodily continuity, as a supposed necessary condition of continuing personal identity, had been maintained. We should have bodies to help the recognition of continuing identity, but we should not have bodily continuity in the sense required if it is to *constitute* our continuing identity.

Thus if we ask what could *constitute* the continuing identity of a man who lives first in this world and then in another, resurrection-doctrines are not much more favourably placed than immortality-doctrines.[1]

Now suppose a theologian wishes to say that the Apostles saw a glorified body. They saw an eschatological reality, Jesus in his heavenly mode of being. If this is what they saw, strict bodily continuity is not merely unnecessary but quite impossible. Flesh and blood cannot inherit the kingdom of God, as St. Paul says, unless you can travel to heaven in precisely the same sense as you can travel to Brighton or to Mars and pay lightning return visits. So that whether or not the tomb was empty is neither here nor there.

And in so far as it is nevertheless maintained that the body the Apostles saw was *strictly* continuous with the one which had lain in the grave, then Jesus is necessarily thought of as having returned to this life we live. That is, the more strictly and literally an Event theory of the resurrection is maintained the more it approximates to the theory of Paulus,

[1] But see also Peter Geach, *God and the Soul* (1969), chapter 2. I am not quite sure where Geach stands on the question whether there *can* be material continuity (in the required sense) *between two worlds*.

that Jesus never really died, but revived in the tomb from a trance, pushed his way out and borrowed the gardener's clothes. A strict Event theory is in practice indistinguishable from Paulus' theory, and if we care to appeal to history it must be said that we do not have very much historical evidence that members of Jesus' immediate circle observed him die, saw his body removed from the cross, and because they assisted at its burial knew where the grave was, and that it was sealed. For what they are worth the narratives we have suggest rather the contrary.

On a strict Event theory the disciples, meeting the risen Jesus, might have said "Oh! we thought they had killed you, but you are not dead after all!" They might have judged him to have *escaped* death: it is not obvious how they could claim that he had conquered death, and could not die again.

So there is a dilemma here. If Jesus' appearance to his disciples is exactly like the appearance of a politician at a party conference then all it can do is falsify the presumption that he was dead. The more literally Jesus' appearances are understood to be this-worldly events the less we can see how they are supposed to give meaning to and to justify the assertion that he lives eternally in a glorified mode of being. So in its strictest form the Event theory must be abandoned. If it had ambitions to satisfy the physicalist doctrine that persisting personal identity is constituted by the body's *uninterrupted* track through space and time it cannot fulfil them and at the same time be of any theological use.

Perhaps it can yet be of theological use if it makes the more modest claim. The Apostles saw—with their eyes—a glorified body. This sight constitutes the historical foundation of Christian faith. It was for the Apostles a verification of the Christian theological beliefs.

In this form the resurrection-doctrine no longer purports to establish spatio-temporal continuity between Jesus' natural body and his resurrection-body. But it does say that for intelligible discourse about life after death we must suppose a recognizable body. Talk of *my* surviving death has no meaning unless the post-mortem me is recognizably *me*, has experiences and can communicate with others. So I shall need to be able to identify others and to be identifiably myself. I shall need, if not "historically" *the same* body as I have now, yet at least *a* recognizable body which may conveniently be thought of as a replica of my present body. And this implies that I shall live in a space-time world.

There are two questions here; first, that of the conceivability of a resurrection-world and second that of the Resurrection-Event, now understood as an anticipatory glimpse of Jesus in the resurrection-world which is thought to validate the Christological beliefs.

The conceivability of another spatio-temporal world discontinuous with ours has been defended in an article by Anthony Quinton in *Philosophy* for 1962. The minimum conditions of intelligible discourse about an after-life have been discussed in various places by Professor H. H. Price and others. The relation of all this to the verification of theological propositions was raised by Professor John Hick in an article in *Theology Today* in 1960 which began an argument which is not ended yet. Material can be found in the *Canadian Journal of Theology*, the *Australasian Journal of Philosophy* and in Hick's own subsequent writings, such as chapter 8 of his *Faith and Knowledge* (second edition 1967). Hick still maintains unaltered his original thesis that theological assertions have factual meaning because they may be verified after death. He allows that on his supposition they cannot be falsified, and he allows that we cannot specify very clearly what the verifying state of affairs will be like. But he says that we can conceive a resurrection-world in which things would be such that it would be unreasonable *not* to believe in God and his goodness.

There is also a useful sketch of a supposable resurrection-world in Austin Farrer's *Saving Belief* (1964).

We shall make use of this material in order to test the

suggestion that the appearances of Jesus after his death might vindicate the Christological beliefs about him. If to see the risen Lord was to enjoy by anticipation a glimpse of the consummation of all things in Christ then this is an instance, perhaps the only one so far, of what Hick calls *eschatological verification*: that is, the verification of a theological proposition by experiencing a religiously unambiguous state of affairs in which it would be unreasonable to disbelieve it.

Pannenberg suggests such a view of the resurrection. Those who saw the risen Jesus momentarily, and in microcosm, saw the end of the world, the final perfectly god-revealing and faith-vindicating state of affairs.

Here we are near to the heart of the Event theory, which is the conviction that the Easter faith is not identical with but is a response to the Easter event. The Resurrection, it is said, is not identical with the birth of the Easter faith and the beginning of the kerygma, but a distinct objective happening as a consequence of which men came to believe the Easter faith. It is customary to quote Paul against Bultmann: "If Christ has not been raised your faith is futile" with the assumption that the text implies that the raising of Christ and the human faith-response to that raising are quite distinct things. People stress strongly the unexpectedness of the Resurrection-Event, particularly as modern criticism has come to regard the use of the Christological titles and the dominical predictions of the resurrection and even of the passion as all originating in the post-Easter period. This linguistic explosion must have been set off by something, it is said. The Resurrection-Event is seen as a bolt from the blue, and as being the ground of belief in the resurrection of Jesus and subsequently the resurrection of Christians. The Resurrection-Event is supposed to be both the historical cause of the rise of Christianity and that which justifies Christian belief.

As it stands this will not do. If the Resurrection-Event were really a bolt from the blue it would not verify anything, for there is no prior expectation to be verified: indeed it would not be intelligible. In the passage just quoted Paul says "If the dead are not raised, then Christ is not raised" (1 Corinthians 15: 16), setting the resurrection firmly in the context of long-held eschatological beliefs: if those beliefs are not true the resurrection-belief is meaningless. And indeed what Paul says in the text quoted seems to fit at least as well with the Theological theory as with any form of Event theory. His argument runs (i) At the end of time the dead will be raised; (ii) Jesus is the eschatological Messiah; (iii) So Jesus is preached as risen from the dead; (iv) You have heard and believed this preaching; (v) How then can you go back and cast doubt upon its major premiss, (i)?

So some kind of eschatological belief-system must be presupposed to make the supposed Resurrection-Event intelligible and theologically productive. The attraction of the suggestions of Quinton, Hick and Farrer is that they propose a conceivable eschatological hypothesis which a Resurrection-Event could then be claimed to verify. Let us set it out.

We can conceive that there should be two physical systems which in no way interact physically. Now space and time are not infinite containers whose bare existence is logically prior to their having any contents. They are simply two orders of relations within a closed physical system. Two quite independent physical systems would not be locatable in a space and time common to them both. Each would have its own space and time, and there would be no causal route from one to the other. It is possible, in a work of fiction, to create another world whose time cannot be fixed on our time-scale and whose place is not continuous with our space. Such a supposition is not meaningless.

Now God is the maker of any world there may be: so suppose him the maker of two worlds, this and another, which are morally related in his design as promise is to fulfilment, as journey is to destination. We live now in one: we hope at last to be reconstituted and live a second life in the other. Here the knowledge of God is riddling and ambiguous, but then all will be as plain as it can be, though admittedly we can only give the barest intimation of what a faith-vindicating state of things will be like.

Now according to Christological belief Jesus was the first man who was so perfectly what men ought to be, and who died away from this world in such perfect relinquishment of all that he was, that he was fittingly reinstated just as he was in the next. It is fitting that his grave should be left empty because his entire life in this world was such that he had nothing to put behind him or to discard. The whole of what he had been was fit for the next world and could be taken up into it. Thus his life exhibits an ideal unity of the two worlds. Ideally this world entire ought to be capable of redemption, assumption into the next. And he is the promise of this.

But if Jesus now lives embodied in glory in another world how can there be apparitions of him to his friends here below in this world? How can immortal reality be seen with mortal eyes? It will be said that we do not know: the thing is unique and must be. But we can see that if the whole reality of what Jesus has been in this world has been assumed into the next then he is not only the most God-suggesting feature of this world's history but also the only accessible and humanly knowable next-worldly entity. Since he still is all he was he can reappear as he was, recognizably the same.

Now the claim is that this myth of another world which we have just made up is not intrinsically absurd, and the Resurrection-Event proved, at least to those who saw it, that it or something very like it is in fact true.

But in this form the Event theory is becoming curiously frail and empty. A speculative hypothesis, if it is to be productive, must be more than barely supposable: there must be some positive reason for entertaining this particular hypothesis, and some knowledge of what states of affairs could verify it. If we are obliged to admit that though the Apostles saw we cannot specify how they saw or what they saw, then we cannot say how their seeing could verify the hypothesis, and appeal to the supposed Resurrection-Event can contribute nothing of significance to the justification of Christological belief. After all, for Paul, that "at the end of time the dead will be raised" was not simply a barely conceivable hypothesis but a theological proposition which he believed to be true. He defended and explained it by theological arguments, whether good or bad. If the eschatological belief-system is reduced to the status of no more than a conceivable hypothesis then we shall find, and we do find, that the Resurrection-Event is being asked to do too much. It is supposed to be describable in this-worldly terms so that ordinary canons of historical evidence can be applied to it and its occurrence can be rendered historically probable: and it is also supposed to verify Christological beliefs. It is supposed to be both open to ordinary sense-perception and to be an eschatological vision. The Apostles are supposed both to see the eschatological glory of Jesus and yet to remain among the number of those who talk by faith, not by sight. In short, the hypothesis of a resurrection-world has been made up in the hope of making the Resurrection-Event intelligible, and the Event thus made intelligible is supposed to return the compliment and verify the hypothesis. It is too arbitrary: several other hypotheses might have been put into the same circular argument.

Wolfhart Pannenberg undoubtedly holds a form of Event theory of the Resurrection. But he strongly criticizes any suggestion that the Christian today can have an immediate experience of the glorified Jesus. There is, he says, no sure way of testing a claim to such an experience, and indeed it is promised, not for the present time, but for the end of the world.[1] But why then make such a claim for the Apostles? How can it be judged by the historian that the Apostles

[1] *Jesus God and Man* (Eng. Trans. 1968), pp. 27f., 112ff.

not merely claimed but were *justified* in claiming to have had such an experience?

Pannenberg has perhaps inherited from his predecessors an odd reluctance to admit that the Christological confessions *Jesus lives!*, *Jesus is Lord!* were originally arrived at by a process of argument. Bultmann makes the kerygma a linguistic miracle, Pannenberg makes the Resurrection-Event a material miracle. I suspect that the theologians' stress on the novelty of the Easter faith as something whose rise is humanly inexplicable is motivated by a desire to strengthen the Beaten-Men Argument. It is said that the Apostles could not have reached the Easter faith by their own resources. But if the task of Christology is to justify the Christological beliefs so far as it can be done (and Pannenberg thinks this) then that must include retracing the arguments by which those beliefs were reached. An appeal to miracle is a confession of failure.

Event theorists try to strengthen their case by introducing circumstantial considerations. Pannenberg is willing to appeal to a form of the Beaten-Men Argument, and to the Empty Tomb. These props are far too weak. Just how weak they are is revealingly exposed in a book by Daniel Fuller, *Easter Faith and History* (1968), who argued that "the resurrection can be established simply by the application of the historical method to the Gentile mission".[1] Here is the proof:

> Since this mission, which is an established fact of history, cannot be explained apart from the motivation of Paul, which must include as a salient fact the consciousness of having received a teaching office from Christ, therefore Paul actually was given a teaching office by the risen Christ.

Even among more sophisticated writers one meets versions of the argument that because Christian beliefs arose unexpectedly and prospered exceedingly they must be true—an observation which leads one to join Wittgenstein in his

[1] p. 228.

reflections upon the remarkable weakness of religious evidences.[1]

It will not do then, to propose an Event theory of the Resurrection as an historical explanation of the rise of Christian beliefs or as a justification of those beliefs—above all not both at once, as is usually done. To say this is not to deny that the Apostles had strange experiences (they may well have done for all we know), but only to say that an Event theory of the Resurrection cannot by itself explain the meaning of and justify Christological beliefs.

So we turn finally to the Theological Theory. Christological statements are framed by applying theological notions to matters of historical fact. The beliefs that Jesus was the Messiah, the Son of Man, the Lord, the Son of God were arrived at by applying some theological ideas current in contemporary Judaism to the known course of Jesus' life and death. So far from the Easter Event creating the Easter faith as is commonly said, it was rather the Easter faith which made the Easter Event possible. For the Easter Event was presumably an apprehension by men of the risen and exalted Jesus. But for men to be able to cognize Jesus in a religious experience they must already have and know how to use the concepts by means of which they are to interpret that experience. The possibility of a recognition of the living Christ in Christian experience *presupposes* good independent theological grounds for believing him risen.

So it is that historically we find that formal theological confessions of Jesus as Risen Lord antedate the picturesque stories describing his appearance to individuals. The popular apologetic has created confusion by reversing the true order. Only after the Christian apologetic has established convincingly the correspondence between the hope of Israel and the course of Jesus' career is it possible for the disciples to recognize the risen Lord in the meal at Emmaus. The epistemology of resurrection-belief is beautifully mapped out

[1] *Lectures & Conversations*, pp. 6of.

in Luke's story.[1] Only because Paul already knows what the Christian belief is is it possible for him to identify the No! on the Damascus road as spoken by the Jesus whom he was proposing to persecute.

The theological groundwork may have been done during Jesus' lifetime, but the sudden efflorescence of Christological beliefs began after his death. This man, it was concluded, must be the Christ. Subsequently Christophanic visions perhaps occurred, and they are in a way Gospels in miniature, for their quasi-bodily features look back, they are drawn from the history of Jesus. The Christophanic vision-story is a shorthand way of saying that Jesus is the Christ of God. It is a story about *Jesus*, seen as the Christ. Subsequently Gospels were written in which historical traditions of Jesus' career are thoroughly revised to express the post-Easter faith.

It was a muddle ever to have thought of the resurrection-faith as springing from a post-mortem event in Jesus' career —a bizarre notion which led to the entanglement of the resurrection with the superstitions we discussed under Psi-theories. It is like the superstition of tying the doctrine of the Incarnation to an antenatal episode in Jesus' career, namely his virginal conception[2] by Mary.

In fact each pericopé in the Gospels preaches the gospel by blending historical episode and christological concept. Every pericopé in a Gospel exhibits Jesus as the Christ of God and so proclaims the resurrection. The whole of a gospel such as Mark's is a resurrection-narrative.

Thus when the Apostles said that in the risen Lord they recognized the same Jesus, the identity here is not the identity of a thing which persists unchanged through a period of time (the post-resurrection Jesus is not in time), but the identity predicated when we assert that Edward Heath is the same man as the Prime Minister. To see Jesus

---

[1] It cannot be emphasized too much that in the New Testament *that Jesus is risen* is proved from the Old Testament.

[2] "The Virgin Birth", a popular misnomer, refers to a different doctrine.

as risen Lord was to see someone who had been an acquaintance as nothing less than Lord and Christ, living and exalted. The myth of a posthumous apparition plays no essential part in this.

The Chalcedonian formula pictures divine and human natures indissolubly conjoined without confusion in the Incarnate Lord Jesus Christ. This is to say in picture-language that Jesus is the fulfilment of Scripture: that is, that in Jesus Christ theological concept is decisively and finally instantiated in contingent fact. Every Christological statement joins divine to human, the hope of Israel and the history of Jesus.

So let us take stock and make clear what we do and do not claim to have shown by our study of the resurrection. We take it that the resurrection-belief is that Jesus of Nazareth is risen from the dead and lives as Christ and Lord of the human race. We have not discussed the truth of this belief, but certain aspects of its meaning and the logic of its justification. In particular we have been considering the claim that the resurrection was something which happened to Jesus after his death. This we may call the Resurrection-Event. It is claimed that the occurrence of this event is historically demonstrable because certain people had experiences perhaps of a rather special kind only explicable upon the assumption that it had occurred. Thus established the Resurrection-Event is supposed to justify the Christological kerygma.

I have criticized this picture—you may think, at inordinate length—for it does not seem to me that we are in a position to say clearly what the supposed Resurrection-Event was (that is, what the appearances of the risen Lord to the disciples were like), or to establish historically either the occurrence of the event or the authenticity of the Apostles' experiences. In any case appeal to the experiences, and the Event they seem to presuppose, does not seem to be necessary to the justification of the resurrection-belief, within the New Testament's thought-world.

For example, St. Paul, explaining the gospel in some hellenistic synagogue, might reason like this: he would argue from the Old Testament about the true character of the expected Messiah and the manner in which God would bring in his kingdom at the end of time. He would try to show that the Messiah must suffer, and he would speak of Jesus, the crucified Messiah, and argue that this man is now made Lord and Christ, the first fruits of a universal harvest. That is, I can imagine him preaching and proving Jesus as crucified and risen Messiah without it being necessary for him to invoke a Resurrection-Event or eyewitness testimony to it. They are, I think, logically superfluous, and were perhaps developed rather in the way the legend of Mary's virginal conception of Jesus was developed, as a picturesque reinforcement.

The doctrines of the incarnation and the resurrection are in truth very similar for the historical matter of each is the whole of Jesus' history. But they have been pulled apart because the former is associated with an antenatal and the latter with a post-mortem legend. So both have become distorted because they have lost the breadth of their proper historical grounding in the entire course of Jesus' career.

The point of the appeal to eyewitnesses was that to those who had known Jesus in the days of his flesh the conviction of his messiahship came with great force. They were those who had seen Jesus and now knew him Lord and Christ. When something long familiar falls into a new pattern, and takes on a new aspect, we naturally describe what we have suddenly come to see as a fresh perception, as Wittgenstein says.[1] It is quite possible that the dawning resurrection-faith gave rise to remarkable resurrection-experiences. But those experiences are logically secondary, not primary. Their historical uncertainty, therefore, is not of very great moment.

[1] *Philosophical Investigations* (1953), pp. 195f.

11

ARGUMENTS FOR THE EXISTENCE OF CHRIST

WE TURN now to study some issues raised by, and arguments employed in contemporary Christian talk about Christ. From early times the term Christ has been employed as a proper name, so our first question concerns the referent of this name. Who precisely *is* this person, Christ, of whom it is claimed that he lives, and can be known? What arguments are advanced in support of the claim that he lives?

The name Jesus Christ is a proper name and we have argued already that every Christological statement makes some reference to Jesus of Nazareth, so that the historical Jesus provides some historical basis for all the various things said about Jesus Christ. When people speak of Jesus Christ as doing this, that or the other, they speak of someone who is the same person as he who walked in Palestine.

However, we have to ask whether all the various functions predicated of Jesus Christ could be fulfilled by one person. For the name "Jesus" does so many jobs. He is indeed the one who walked in Palestine, but he is also the one who lives in heaven, the one who acts in certain ways in the world, figures in certain documents, lives in certain hearts. How can all these hang together in one man? There is a certain overloading here which is already apparent even as early as St. Paul's letters. Jesus is particular and individual but Paul talks of Christ in universal and corporate idioms.[1] Just how Paul is to be understood here is a highly controversial matter, but we can sufficiently make our point by

[1] Surveyed in C. F. D. Moule, *The Phenomenon of the New Testament* (1967), Chap. II.

saying that on at least *some* of the occasions where Paul uses the term "Christ" the name "Jesus" cannot very comfortably be substituted for it.

It is of course true that we speak of "the Crown" or "the Queen" or "Regina" in many contexts where it would not be very appropriate to substitute the name "Elizabeth". It is the Crown rather than Elizabeth which prosecutes and pardons, owns Estates, approves Acts of Parliament, bestows Commissions in the Armed Forces and so on. In referring to the Crown and what it does we use a neuter pronoun. But in the case of Jesus it does not seem right to think of him as embedded in an institutional setting and surrounded by a bureaucracy which does all manner of things in his name, according to rules. The individual Jesus is, as it were, thought of as personally involved whenever Christ is spoken of. The historical personage and the infinite and universal person are the same person. Hence our uncomfortable feeling that a certain overloading has taken place. More predicates have been attached to Jesus than can possibly be borne by a single individual.

The sufficiency of our historical knowledge of Jesus is a different question, and perhaps an easier one. It can be expressed thus: in view of the notorious uncertainties of our historical knowledge of this man can we be reasonably clear that the name picks out unmistakably a specific individual? In the case of many New Testament figures we are very unsure. Take the name John. We can without much difficulty hive off and keep together a bundle of historical statements associated with the name of John the Baptist. But then there remains a large body of other referring phrases, such as

    (i) The son of Zebedee;
    (ii) The beloved disciple;
    (iii) The fourth evangelist;
    (iv) The "theologian" referred to in the Apocalypse;
and (v) The elder.

And we do not know how to group these phrases together.

We simply do not know whether (i) and (ii), or (iii) and (v) refer to the same individual.

The case of Jesus does not seem to be as difficult as this. It is more on a level with the case of John the Baptist. His name can be incorporated into a body of historical statements which together define a specific historical individual and say something of what manner of man he was.

For the purposes of Christian belief such a body of historical statements would need to be sufficiently definite and well established to make recognition possible after all this time and in very different circumstances. Whether we have such a body of statements is for historians to say. Notice that we do not need to make every item in the collection very highly probable. A body of historical statements makes up a kind of web, and the breaking of a few threads in a web does not destroy the entire web. A few errors in a biography do not make it a life of somebody else. It is a historical question what sort of web of information about Jesus we can construct: but how we can use the web in order to identify the living Jesus Christ in present-day religious experience is a matter which at least partly involves philosophy.

When we are talking of the referent of the name Jesus Christ the principal problem is not so much whether or not we have adequate historical knowledge of Jesus but rather how all the various predicates attached to the Lord Jesus Christ could all be borne by a single individual. It is not surprising that in so many modern theologies the lines tying talk of Christ down to the historical Jesus of Nazareth have been cut. This does effect a very convenient simplification. Christ becomes a metaphysical principle, the universal form of relation between the Divine and human spirits. The bottleneck caused by routing all traffic between earth and heaven through a single man is removed. However we have argued that this will not do. All talk of Christ is talk of one who is the same person as Jesus of Nazareth.

But the overloading-problem then becomes very serious.

170

As an example of it, consider the extraordinary reference-range of the term "the Body of Christ" in theological talk. It is used to designate the body which was crucified, the collective body of all Christians living and dead, the risen body of Jesus in heaven, and the Eucharistic elements!

Again, in popular preaching the faithful are often directed to treat each occasion of meeting a fellow-man as an occasion of meeting Christ. We should learn to see Christ, to "recognize" him in our neighbour. But if I can "recognize" Christ in *any* man then "Christ" is no more than a name for human nature, concrete universal humanity. To "recognize" Christ in every man can only be to recognize—i.e. acknowledge—the humanity of every man. In this line of talk Jesus Christ is no longer a particular man distinct from others. But in Christological talk he is *both* a particular man *and* universal humanity!

After the Christological debates in the early Church it has become customary to list all the various predicates attached to the name Jesus Christ in two classes, a list of human predicates and a list of divine predicates. Consider for example the various Christophanic visions reported in the New Testament—I mean by this, apparitions of Jesus in glory such as the Transfiguration, the Resurrection Appearances and the Ascension. They combine two elements, divine and human. The divine is a cloud, a radiance, a blinding structureless majesty, unapproachable and un-thinkable. The human is the lineaments of a particular man, Jesus. A Christophanic vision of Jesus in glory unites the two, it is a vision of a man in a cloud. The combination is extraordinary: in a particular man is seen the structureless radiance of eternity, in a blinding cloud is seen the face of a particular man. The two symbols, the man and the cloud, are inseparably conjoined, yet remain distinct.

The coherence of Christian talk about Christ would be easier to grasp if we could fix its *present* reference. So we will begin by considering six arguments by which theologians might try to establish the present existence of the Lord

Jesus Christ. They may be compared with the arguments for the existence of God.[1] Even if, like those latter arguments, they are flawed they may still be useful as indicators; they may throw light on the problem of meaning.

To speak of Christ as "living" need not, perhaps, entail attributing to him the sort of life which interests biologists. He may be living in the sense of being active, keeping "in touch" with his followers. Thus most of the following arguments will be *causal arguments*. Certain phenomena, it is claimed, are caused by Christ, and so are evidence of his present activity. However, the first argument is perhaps more like the Ontological Argument.

1. Sometimes it is argued that the term "the risen Lord Jesus Christ" simply denotes the Christian phenomenon as a whole. The Church is the resurrection: Jesus died and the Church rose. It may be said that Christians are "so many Christs", in the patristic phrase. The Church is a prolongation of the incarnation: in it too the Divine indwells the human. So it is claimed that the present referent of the name "Jesus Christ" can be indicated by pointing to the Church. "Jesus lives" can be analysed as "the Church exists".

This is clearly fallacious, for it would make nonsense of such statements as "Christ indwells Christians", "Christ loves the Church" or "Christ is Lord of the Church" to claim that in them the term "the Church" can be substituted for "Christ". "Christ loves the Church" does not mean the same as "the Church loves the Church". The theory gains such plausibility as it has by incorporating Christological concepts into the definition of the Church, but those concepts are empty unless they have some application distinct from the Church.

Furthermore such a theory of the reference of the name

---

[1] See A. Durwood Foster Jr., "Theological Arguments for Christ's Historicity: Parallels with the Theistic Proofs", in W. R. Farmer, C. F. D. Moule and R. R. Niebuhr, *Christian History and Interpretation* (1967), pp. 57–100. But Foster is concerned with Jesus, not Christ.

Christ must cut its links with Jesus. For "Jesus" is the name of a man, yet on this showing "Jesus lives" cannot be more than a metaphorical way of saying "The Church exists and treasures a memory of Jesus".

2. The second argument is that *from the origin of Christianity*. The Christian beliefs, it is claimed, are so remarkable that no merely natural explanation of their origin can suffice. There was nothing in the circumstances of the disciples adequate to explain the rise among them of so marvellous a faith. This argument is merely a more general form of the Beaten-Men Argument which we have often met already, and we need spend no more time upon it.

3. The third argument also claims to begin from an empirical premiss, in this case *the Church's early expansion, its survival of persecution, its prosperity and its continuation to the present day*. No merely natural explanation of these facts is adequate. Jesus Christ must live and supervise the Church's life. Sometimes this argument is presented in a form similar to the "madman/impostor or Messiah" dilemma-argument for the authenticity of Jesus' claims. Either the whole thing has been a gigantic hoax, or it is genuine. There is an analogous argument too from religious experience, to the effect that the great mystics cannot plausibly be regarded as all impostors or deluded.

Among evangelicals the argument is presented in the form of an exhortation: you can demonstrate that Jesus Christ is alive and powerful by the zeal and persistence of your witness to him. The early Christians proved the resurrection in such a way, and so should we. The central concept here is that of *marturia*, witness even to death.

There is here, then, a very large class of arguments in all of which it is claimed that there is a valid inference from "one or more people believe *p* in a manner *m*" to "*p* is true". And of course there is not. It does not matter what you substitute for *m*, whether the believing be profitable, zealous, fervent, persistent, manifestly sane, sincere or whatever, the argument remains incomplete. Even those who use it would themselves be reluctant to accept the validity of a similar argument for the truth of the beliefs of another successful religion.

Locke (I think) has somewhere a revealing aside to the effect that even a Turk will die for his religion, though his is a false religion. Not even a man's willingness to die for his beliefs can show his beliefs to be true, though it certainly does show that he is sincere in holding them.

4. The fourth argument, a rather similar one, is a *moral argument from certain distinctively Christian moral virtues*. In its cruder form this argument simply claims that some moral virtues conspicuous among Christians are evidence of the power of Christ at work in their lives. Such Christians witness to him by the way in which they do not claim their virtue as their own achievement, but constantly attest that they owe everything to Christ. And so if a Christian's virtue is conspicuous enough and if he can successfully persuade us that it is in no way his own achievement but the work in him of another, he may persuade us that the grace of the living Christ has taken hold of him.

This argument is difficult to formalize. Does it require a general proposition to the effect that the religious beliefs of good men are true and the religious beliefs of bad men are false? Or, more modestly, is there a claim here that the better a man is the more nearly true his beliefs are? Or, more cautiously still, is there a claim that the better a man is the more reasonable it is to accept his own account of himself and of what makes him a good man? It is not easy to see how any of these propositions could be proved. If believing the true religion is part of what counts as being a good man then the general proposition that the religion of good men is true is tautologous: but if not, then it seems to be false. For good men seem to be in as much disagreement about matters of religion as the rest of us. As for the last proposition suggesting that we ought to accept a good man's account of himself, I see many reasons for being sceptical about people's own explanations of themselves.

And how can a man increase his own efforts to the point at which it is evident that they are not his own?

A more elaborate version of this moral argument runs as follows:

  (i) Jesus introduced into the world a new moral quality q;

  (ii) q cannot be exhibited by ordinary men by their own unaided efforts. In the old technical language it is supernatural and cannot be *acquired*, but must be *infused*, received by grace;

  (iii) Yet q has been continuously exhibited in the Church by at least some of its members, right down to the present day;

  (iv) Therefore, Jesus still lives in the Church, and inspires the quality of q in some or all of its members.

By their fruits ye shall know them. A man, a church, proves that Christ lives by being Christ-like. The value commonly assigned to q is self-giving love, *agapé*. Men are naturally self-centred or at least very much concerned about themselves and self-preservation: so that where there is a spirit which is altogether without thought of self there is the spirit of Christ.

But again the argument is incomplete. The marvellousness and rarity of this quality of character is not in dispute, but it is less easy to prove that it is specific to Christians so that a direct connection with Christ can be demonstrated for each instance where it is displayed. How, without begging the question, can it be shown that a certain moral quality is supernatural so that its presence can *only* be due to divine assistance? How can we set about fixing the limits of what can be done without divine grace? How can we experimentally set up a situation from which it has been excluded? If an argument of this kind is to prove the living reality of Christ it must do more than show that each and every man who is q has drawn inspiration from Jesus: it must show that he could never be q merely by trying to be like Jesus, so that if he is q he can be so only by Jesus Christ's help.

The argument from distinctive moral qualities supplies a neat example of the dangers of trying to have it both ways. Where there is agapé, there is Christ—so goes the maxim, but is the maxim itself synthetic or analytic? When a confessed Christian exhibits agapé, then this may be taken as evidence of the synthetic truth of the maxim. But when a Gandhi touches the untouchables in a most Christlike manner the maxim is treated as analytic in order to claim his act for Christ. In classical theology there was often a similar manœuvre in order to avoid the bald assertion that there cannot be a virtuous pagan. If he is virtuous he must be an implicit Christian. But this is to define virtuous pagans out of existence, not to show there are none.

5. The difficulty here of showing that Christ is the only possible cause of some phenomenon can also be urged against the fifth argument, that from *the creativity and power of renewal in the Christian tradition,* which is often used as evidence of the activity of the spirit of Christ. Yes, people say, the Church has in many periods of its history been stagnant or even evil, but it has a wonderful power of recovery. New life is breathed into dry bones, and the humanly impossible happens. The influence of Christ upon the Church is not just a matter of historical tradition, like the influence of Nelson upon the British Navy. It is a living influence, the influence of one *who is in touch* and who does new things all the time. Christ has left a pattern, but the pattern is not repeated over and over unchanged, as a gramophone record always plays the same tune. On the contrary, in the Christian tradition new ways of being Christ-like are constantly being discovered. If Christ were dead there would remain only the one way of being Christlike in the world, namely Jesus' own way. But he is alive, and perpetually finds new ways of expressing himself.

But once again the argument is incomplete. Imagine an Admiral conducting a naval engagement. At Dartmouth all his dreams were of Nelson, and so now his conduct of the engagement is along lines reminiscent of Nelson's strategy. Nelson's influence may be called creative, for the Admiral, instead of slavishly copying his exemplar, perhaps does something which Nelson never did. Indeed, the resources at his disposal nowadays being very different from those at Nelson's disposal, what he does *must* be different from what Nelson did, yet perhaps we might still regard his action as faithful to the spirit of Nelson. But what *could* he do which would really justify us in saying that Nelson is still alive and inspiring him? How can we draw a clear line between being in the metaphorical sense inspired by the spirit of Nelson and being in some much stronger sense inspired by the spirit of Nelson? By what criteria could we surely distinguish between a case of the former and a case of the latter?

It is true that the Church *directs* believers to refer certain aspects of their experience to Christ as cause. In sermons believers are directed to see Christ in the face of the vagrant, they are directed to refer to Christ experiences of being forgiven, of the power of love, or of successfully vanquishing a temptation. But this is a *direction* to impose a certain pattern upon experience, to see things in a certain way. Whereas our present argument is claiming that the pattern rises *a posteriori*, from experience. It is arguing not that certain experiences *ought* to be viewed under a certain pattern, but that certain experiences *can* only be viewed under a certain pattern. And this can't be done.

6. The sixth argument is that which a man might frame *by way of interpreting to himself his own experience of conversion.* So, in describing it, I shall use the first person singular. Let us suppose, then, that I have an experience of forgiveness and moral renewal. A day or two ago I was in a state of turmoil. I was inwardly divided against myself and so unable to grasp any solid possession of myself *vis-à-vis* the outer world. Everything within and without me was chaotic and hostile. I was oppressed by a sense of meaninglessness, moral failure and indifferent malignity. Either my life had no meaning or its meaning was such an unpleasant joke as

to be intolerable. I felt doomed, outcast and accursed. But then something miraculous happened. Perhaps through reading the New Testament, or by hearing someone speak about Christ, or during a church service, or perhaps while driving a car alone in the rain, or walking over grass in the morning, I suddenly receive an overwhelming impression of bliss, tranquillity, and reinstatement. I am altogether lifted out of and removed an infinite distance away from my old self and its straitjacket of dread and guilt. The old horrors have gone to the bottom of the sea. Naked as a babe, I know myself freely and entirely accepted and rehabilitated. My life changes, I am morally renewed. Even though the old storms will surely blow again I know now that they can never entirely uproot me. I shall have the trick of bending with them now that I am rooted in the eternal and immovable, borne up by everlasting arms.

There is no doubt that such experiences do take place. We can read about them in William James[1] and elsewhere. And very often the context in which such an experience takes place, and the thoughts which run across the experient's mind at the time, strongly suggest to him that he refer his experience to God in Christ. He is saved, and Jesus Christ is his saviour.

Now the language in which the experience is described is psychological language about private experience. How can the experient justifiably refer his experience to an objective cause outside himself?

He might argue by analogy relying on historical knowledge of Jesus. He might say, "The way I have experienced salvation is recognizably like the way in which other people experienced salvation long ago in Palestine. The Gospels may not contain material for a biography of Jesus, they may tell us nothing of his inner life, but at least they do tell us what it was like to meet him when in need and to experience in his person the good news of God's imminent reign, his saving power and love. In so far as I have experienced the

[1] *The Varieties of Religious Experience* (1902).

178

same thing that the Gospel-writers tell of, I have good reason to believe that I have encountered one and the same saviour".

By this account the convert has explained to us how it is that he regards his own experience as an experience of the living Christ. But, once again, the experience of salvation is not peculiar to Christianity. What seem to be very similar experiences are susceptible of interpretation by quite different conceptual systems—psychotherapy, nature-mysticism and other religions. And there are political conversions nowadays too. It is hard to see how a religious experience could come to one so labelled that it could only be interpreted in one way.

We have now considered six lines of argument by which theology might attempt to prove the present existence and activity of Jesus Christ. I suggested that they might be compared with the arguments for the existence of God, but they are in some ways weaker. The proofs of God begin with, or purport to begin with, matters of empirical fact—the bare existence of the world, or some rather general features of it, such as the intelligibility of the natural order, the contingency of things, or the possibility of the moral life. The proofs of Christ have to begin by asserting that some phenomenon is supernatural, or is not explicable in ordinary terms. Our six arguments began from (i) the existence of the Church, (ii) the circumstances of its origin, (iii) its expansion and continuance, (iv) Christian moral virtues, (v) the creativity of the Christian tradition, and (vi) conversion. In each case they had to maintain that we were dealing here with something extraordinary and surpassing what is humanly possible. The manner in which the phenomenon was extraordinary then had to be matched up against Jesus in some way in order to establish the reference to him. It *is* extraordinary in the sort of way he *was* extraordinary. For example, Christians love as Jesus loved, their loving is extraordinary in just the way his was, so that it is reasonable to conclude that he still lives and fills them with his love.

Or, a second example, the Church, with its Lord, undergoes experiences of defeat and recovery, loss and gain, dying and rising like his, in solidarity with him, and so it reveals his presence in it.

The arguments are incomplete. This is not to say that a man who has experienced conversion is wrong to claim that Jesus Christ is his Saviour, or even that he is unreasonable in claiming that Jesus Christ is his Saviour. He may be right for all we know, but he has not *proved* that he is right. He may have shown that the phenomena *can* be interpreted this way, but not that they must be.

We said that the arguments for the existence of Christ, though flawed, might yet throw light on the problem of meaning. Our consideration of them has illustrated the way in which Christian believers refer their experience to Christ. There is a voluntary element here, in that the Church collectively encourages its members so to interpret their experience. By an act of will the body of Christians posit Jesus Christ as their Lord and see in him one who lives and is active in the world. They could be right, but they have not proved they are, at any rate by the arguments we have considered.

There is a similar incompleteness about an argument which seeks to answer the question, where is Jesus Christ now? He is a man, he lives, yet he is invisible: so where is he? We can call this argument *the argument from different moral worlds* and express it as follows: "Living" is an analogical notion, more like *travelling*, which can be done in several different ways, than like *bicycling*, which can be done in only one way. There are different ways of living, and indeed we talk of different ways of life. It is possible for somebody's style of life to be so radically different from my own that I can only speak of him as living in a quite different world. There can be an alarming strangeness about a man of superlative moral goodness or creative gifts: he seems to have his eyes on things we cannot see.

Now it is possible to leap from one moral world to another

by undergoing a conversion. If one does this one can only describe the new state of being in odd and vehement idioms, like the language of lovers and the language of miracle. Lovers walk on air, Jesus is seen walking on water. In the same way Plato points out that to leave the Cave and face the sun requires a radical revision of concepts. The very meanings of words are different.

Could one then imagine a moral realm so exalted, and requiring so complete a transformation of the self to make entry into it possible, that it would be right to speak of it as being like a different world? Socrates would have thought it obvious that the philosopher who would attain truth must become an ascetic: one of his least congenial doctrines to modern philosophers. But perhaps he was right?

Now when the theologians speak about heaven, the place where God is and where Jesus Christ lives, they do not mean that it is a kind of second physical world as we were imagining in a fantasy about the resurrection. Jesus is not like Uncle George on the astral plane. He is invisible to sense not so much because he has been removed to a metaphysical world, but rather because he is morally exalted over this world. Why can he not be seen? Not so much for the reason that the furniture in the next room cannot be seen as rather in the way that a moral truth can be so obvious that no one adverts to it, or in the way that the music of the spheres was supposed to be inaudible because it was resounding all the time. To understand what religious truth is consider those things which are so obvious as to be unseen, and consider too how a change of viewpoint may suddenly bring forward what had previously been unnoticed. "I can't see what she sees in him," people say, but perhaps it is there even though they cannot see it.

Incompleteness remains however. There are men so good their goodness goes quite unnoticed, but I have never met anyone so good that he himself was invisible. There are men so self-forgetful, or so mortified by asceticism that death holds no terrors for them, but not men of whom it would be nonsense to say that they are dead. There are truths so obvious that we neglect them, but in principle they can be made obvious to all, they can be publicly pointed out. Mary can specify what she sees in Richard and may be proved right: if not, love really *is* blind.

And so if there really is another moral world in which the reality of Jesus Christ is *evident* then those who inhabit it ought in principle to be able to share their knowledge and make public what they see. They ought to be able to specify what experiences are to count as experiences of meeting him, what events are to count as instance of his working, without too much disagreement among themselves.

Christians claim to "know" Christ, and such knowledge may be mediate or immediate. If it is mediate, it is gained discursively, by reasoning. We have been considering a number of the trains of reasoning by which it might be hoped to establish that Jesus Christ lives, and is real today. They seem incomplete. But what about the possibility of immediate knowledge of Jesus Christ, by acquaintance with him? It deserves study, because claims of this kind are certainly made, and it could be argued plausibly that a man who claims immediate acquaintance with Christ is not in so difficult a position as a man who claims to have met God. God is by definition both infinite and simple. He presents no structure for the mind to grasp, so that it is indeed very hard to see how one could specify what an experience of meeting God could possibly be like.

But Jesus is a particular man, so the claim that one is acquainted with him is not quite so puzzling and obscure. Besides, the older empiricist theory of knowledge, from Locke to Russell, was by general consent not at its strongest in handling our knowledge of other persons. It began within the self, and seemed to suggest that our friends are logical constructions, mere inferred entities of which we have rather fragmentary analogical knowledge. Yet this was obviously unsatisfactory and many notable voices, including those of

Cook Wilson, Webb and Macmurray, have been raised against it. A child obviously knows its mother long before it knows itself. And does this not suggest that our knowledge of other persons is more than a construction from the information picked up by our organs of sense? Do not these considerations encourage us to explore the possibility of immediate knowledge of other people? In the case of immediate knowledge of Jesus Christ sensible signs are not wholly cut away (that *would* be risky) for we have historical knowledge of Jesus as a guide and safeguard against arbitrariness. Is it possible that with its aid communion with him may be had in a way like that in which with the help of our eyes and ears we can commune with our contemporaries?

12

CLAIMS TO "KNOW" CHRIST

WHAT, THEN, are we to say of claims to "know" Christ: claims, that is, that the referent of the name Jesus Christ is given immediately in occasions of acquaintance with him?

Undoubtedly talk of knowing Christ plays a prominent part in Christian language, especially in Protestantism. It is considered very important "really" to know Christ, to have a "personal" or a "saving" knowledge of him. At the time of writing a local church is displaying a vast poster which says "Life can be so much richer when you know Jesus Christ. DO YOU KNOW CHRIST? This church exists to make him known". We have, I think, all been puzzled by such talk, and perhaps embarrassed. The embarrassment is an indirect witness to the realism of the idioms in which people talk to us of knowing Christ. What they attest is nothing less than an intense and intimate personal fellowship, such as Englishmen do not discuss in public.

I have suggested that we ought to be willing to take such language seriously in spite of its obvious philosophical difficulties. Most of us, I suppose, are deeply influenced by philosophical empiricism: but it is widely acknowledged that in that tradition the problem of our knowledge of other people was never very satisfactorily treated. Ever since Descartes it has been common to talk as if we had a peculiarly intimate and privileged knowledge of ourselves, and other people are problematic.

The suggestion seemed to be that I learn from myself, the only person of whom I have immediate knowledge, what it is to be amused or annoyed, and then, on discerning in others what from my own behaviour I have learnt are the physical concomitants of these states, by analogy I ascribe amusement or annoyance to them. It all seems a bit odd, and commonsense and the observation of children strongly suggests the exact opposite, namely that we learn about ourselves by looking at others. Indeed in many contexts we speak of self-knowledge as "learning to see ourselves as others see us", which plainly suggests that it is secondary.

In a British Academy lecture in 1930 the late C. C. J. Webb argued strongly for what he called a "spiritual rapport" between persons.[1] He did not think it would ever be possible to construct our knowledge of one another by inference and analogies out of a supposed original solipsism and the kind of knowledge we have of physical objects.

It sounds very reasonable. After all, biologically men are not solitary rational beings who have formed voluntary associations, but gregarious animals out of whose originally collective, tribal consciousness individual self-awareness has developed.

But Webb added a caution. Such "spiritual rapport", he said, is at least ordinarily mediated by physical signs—the bodily appearance of a person, his writing, or his voice on the telephone. Webb thought it logically possible that there might be entirely non-physical communication between persons, but he insisted that the more the physical mediation is refined away the more precarious and unverifiable becomes the inference to the presence and activity of another person.

Substantially the same point has been made by R. W. Hepburn in criticizing theologies of encounter—that is to say claims that there can be an immediate communion between God and men.[2]

In Christian talk about "knowing Christ" we find that the danger of arbitrary claims and the need for empirical

[1] Reprinted in J. N. Findlay (ed.), *Studies in Philosophy* (1966), pp. 25–39.
[2] *Christianity and Paradox* (1958), pp. 24–59.

controls is recognized. Christ is cognized, it is claimed, with the aid of concepts derived from the New Testament; concepts which are ultimately *a posteriori* because derived from the impact of Jesus of Nazareth upon his contemporaries. And there are other controls: if a man's claim to know Christ is to be generally accepted he must live what is generally understood to be a regenerate life. Furthermore it is acknowledged that human judgement in these matters is fallible. The true Church is invisible, and no mortal can specify its membership with certainty. It is possible for the very elect to be deceived.

These qualifications amount to an admission that though there are some tests the assertion that Smith knows Christ cannot be completely verified by another person, though it is often claimed that Smith himself can be justly sure that he knows Christ. However, this assurance is itself regarded as supernaturally imparted and therefore presumably cannot be completely explicated.

Claims to know Christ are then made subject to certain qualifications: but even so we may well feel that they have gone too far. There seem to be two main classes of difficulty: where is the exalted Jesus to be located—where is he, what status can be assigned to him?—and, in the second place, how can the use of the word "knowledge" in such a context be justified?

Where Christ is to be located is a very difficult question, so difficult that some people will say no more than that believers now can still take up the sort of religious attitudes that Jesus took up; God can be believed, trusted, called Father, obeyed, as Jesus did these things. Jesus opened up a way in which the believer may yet relate himself to God. This way led him to death and yet, it is believed, to vindication in or beyond death. Thus talk of Jesus Christ as living yet means no more than that God can still be trusted as Jesus trusted him. Knowing Jesus Christ can mean only entering into and discovering "for real" the kind of faith in God that Jesus pioneered.

It may be admitted that this is a reductive analysis, which conveys rather less than people wish to convey when they talk of knowing the living Christ. But though the analysis is economical, it may be held to convey all that people can *justifiably* assert when they talk of knowing the living Christ. There may be more to it: we don't know; but this is all that can be said clearly.

Others will suggest, in a rather similar vein, that Jesus Christ is a conceptual entity. He exists as a moral ideal, as exerting an influence upon his disciples. He lives where people read of him, speak of him, celebrate him and live like him.

Again, this is a very parsimonious analysis, conveying much less than people are trying to convey (whether justifiably or not) when they talk of the Living Christ. In such an account the believer gives life to Christ, rather than Christ to the believer. It can be said that "we know him" but scarcely that "he knows us"; that "he belongs to us, we claim him and lay hold of him" but scarcely that "we belong to him, he claims us and lays hold of us". Many Christians will say that a merely exemplary Christ is stone dead. Philosophical understanding, trusting in reason, "the devil's whore", can only arrive at a diabolical caricature of faith. All in it that is response to grace, to divine initiative, is cut away and all that is left is a human aspiration after a dead model.

Another suggestion is that Christ is to be sought through a kind of transformation of our cognitive powers. Through a conversion of the mind we may learn to see familiar persons and things under new patterns. We may learn to see things we never dreamt were there. When the doors of perception have been cleansed there will be no difficulty. The red of the rose in the rain will simply *be* the blood of Christ. The wheat will be obviously orient and immortal. Here faith is being compared with aesthetic imagination as certain romantics have understood it.

Some suggest that the risen Christ lives in another world,

the after-world, which is physically discontinuous with this. There are moral bonds between the two worlds—through prayers in the communion of saints—and though Jesus' proper home is now in the other world he can communicate with people in this world through visions, revelations, sacraments, answers to prayer and so on.

It is of course possible to conceive another world, but unprofitable unless it is of interest to us. Some contact between the worlds is important, but is it thinkable? The problem is like that Descartes faced: if thought and extension are qualitatively different by what kind of levers can the immaterial ghost operate the material machine? If there is another world, how it is possible to detect the points at which the two worlds meet?

Finally, it may be said that Jesus Christ is where God is. We need not seek to locate him in our space, or in another space, nor in the worlds of poetic imagination or moral ideals. He simply is where God is, is what God is, for he is, in the phrase of Karl Barth, "the knowability of God". Where is he then?—simply between men and God, in men and in God. He exists where the human mind thinks God, the heart loves God, the will obeys him. He is not in place, but nor is he in another world: he is omnipresent to every place in the way God is.

Of these five explanations two are reductive, and three at least obscure—including the last, to which I incline. We may well ask, how can the use of the word "knowledge" in such a context be justified? Surely philosophy, supported to a large extent by commonsense, confines the word "knowledge" to cases where the matter known is perfectly evident, and we know that we cannot possibly be mistaken. No religion can claim that the truth of its doctrines is unmistakably evident, for it must surely be allowed that conscientious and "knowing" disbelief are always possible in relation to any religious doctrine whatever. No religion can claim that *any* of its doctrines are quite *undeniable*. Thus while religious believers certainly do make very free use of such words as "knowledge" and "truth" they cannot possibly be justified in so doing.

At this point it is customary to reply that what the Greek and philosophical tradition means by *knowing* is a very different thing from what the Hebrew and theological tradition means.

The distinction is made like this: For Plato knowledge proper, *epistēmē*, is a God's-eye view of the universe, an intellectual vision simple, total and complete in which the mind sees all things in the light of the Good, and sees that all is well. Plato places this vision at the summit of an elaborate hierarchy—sense-perception, reasonable belief, discursive reasoning, rational intuition. It corresponds roughly to what Spinoza, in his more tidy and economical system, calls "intuitive knowledge", the third kind of knowledge.

But for the biblical tradition knowledge is above all a moral concept. We have English idioms which express this: "You ought to have known better," "knowing right from wrong" and the use of "knowingly" or "wittingly" to qualify actions as deliberate and so culpable. So knowledge in the biblical tradition means above all a moral fellowship of persons. Whereas the philosophical tradition attends principally to knowing-that, the rational knowing which takes a proposition for its object, the biblical tradition attends mainly to the kind of knowing which takes a person and the moral claim he makes for its object.

Thus the certainty of religious knowledge consists not in the intellectual adequacy with which believers comprehend God in Christ, but in the unshakeable love and loyalty with which the believer and the one believed in cleave to each other.

So put, the distinction is obviously overdrawn. Both for Plato and for Spinoza the supreme kind of knowledge has much to do with ethics. For both of them knowledge is in a way an eschatological concept: it is a condition which lies at the end of an ascetical journey, as in the theological tradition, where faith is to knowledge as present to future. For both philosphers and theologians the state of knowing is a contemplation of what is truly real and it is a state of blessedness.

So the distinction is overdrawn. Hebrew and Greek are not so far apart: Spinoza belongs to both traditions.

But there is another distinction which is more to the point. The philosophers have tended to concentrate upon knowing-that. The principal truth-conditions for "S knows that p" are usually regarded as being something like this:

1. S holds that p;
2. S is subjectively certain that p, he is quite sure;
3. p is true;

and 4. S has fully adequate reasons for holding that p.

Now some philosophers have thought that the only fully adequate reason for holding that p is that p is analytic, so that not-p is logically impossible. This in effect prices knowledge right out of the market. If only trivial propositions can pass the test of what is to count as knowledge the conditions have been made absurdly stiff.

So perhaps they can be relaxed. Perhaps some synthetic, empirical propositions can slip by, provided that their meaning is perfectly determinate and they can be unambiguously verified, so that they can be called practically indubitable. If we can as it were "see" the state of affairs which plainly makes a proposition true we can as good as see directly the truth of the proposition. We have knowledge.

Hence arises a preference for simple observation-statements, and the ideal of an exhaustive knowledge of the world analysable into simple observation-statements: in a word, epistemological atomism.

Now notice: nothing mysterious can be known, for knowing is plain seeing. If everything can be known, nothing can be mysterious. All that is, all states of affairs, are perfectly specific and so completely specifiable in language. In principle we can know all, and articulate all we know. Everything is clear and distinct and can in principle be expressed as clearly and distinctly as Descartes could wish—perhaps not in our present language, but certainly in a properly-constructed language.

Here is the basic epistemological assumption of the Enlightenment. It leads straight to determinism, and of course also to atheism. When Kant proposed to "destroy knowledge" it was knowledge so conceived that he had in mind. For the obscure problems of religious knowledge simply cannot be handled in such a brilliant light. Nor can the problems of our knowledge of persons.

At one time this rationalist ideal of knowledge seemed obvious, and it still does to many people. But it is worth noticing how very metaphysical it is—that is, how very different it is from the way we use the word "know" and its cognates in ordinary language. And I suggest that in order to throw light on what is meant by talk of knowing Christ we begin by examining some of the idioms in which we speak of knowing people. The alleged distinction between Greek and Hebrew notions of knowledge is not very much to the point. But the distinction between eighteenth-century popular rationalism and ordinary language is.

When we speak of knowing a thing we usually have in mind a complex individual such as a person, a place, a book or a work of art. The basic idea is clearly direct and first-hand experience such as qualifies one to be a witness, and to speak about that which one *knows for oneself*.

The tests of whether a man knows de Gaulle or Paris include

(i) the ability to recognize without hesitation ("Would you know him if you saw him again?");

(ii) a slightly different idea, the ability to identify, pick out or distinguish from others ("I'd know him anywhere", that is, I could pick him out from any setting; "I don't *know him from* Adam");

and (iii) the ability to describe in greater or less detail, especially in the case of "*knowing well*" as opposed to merely "*knowing of*".

For example:

> "Do you know Percy?"
> "Yes—well, I've met him from time to time."
> "Do you happen to *know where* he lives?"
> "No, I am afraid I don't *know* him all that *well*."

To *know* where or when is to be able to *specify* where or when.
Again:

> "Do you know Percy?"
> "Never actually met him, but of course *I know of* him by repute and I know a lot about him. I'm pretty sure I'd know him if I saw him."

Similarly, one might speak of knowing Kant, understanding Kant, having a good knowledge of Kant, knowing how his mind works, and of studying him so deeply that he almost becomes an acquaintance.
Again:

> "She stepped off the train, and though I had not met her for years I knew her at once."
> "I had never met her before, but I felt I knew her at once."
> "I had never met her before, but I knew straight away who she was."

And finally:

> "Do you know the one about the commercial traveller?"
> "Yes, but I've forgotten it, I've forgotten the details, do refresh my memory. I will know it, I'll recognize it when you tell it, it will come back to me."

Notice that we can and often do know unconsciously. At this moment I know that I know Wordsworth's sonnet upon Westminster Bridge, although I can't recall a single line from it. But I know that I will recognize it when I look it up. More than that, I know that if you try to persuade me that a certain line comes from that sonnet though in fact it does not you will not succeed.

The same is true of melodies. Often I know that I know a certain melody, but cannot recall it. I know *that* I know it, but I cannot express *what* I know. Sometimes I can know something without even knowing that I know it. In Paul Bowles' novel *The Sheltering Sky* Kit suddenly realizes that her husband knows that she has been unfaithful to him, but that he doesn't know that he knows it.[1] This knowledge, which he does not know he has, affects his behaviour, and she notices this: indeed she fosters it because it has created a shift in their relationship and a fresher understanding between them. She is pleased about this, for the fact that she understands their present relationship better than he does means that she is in control and will not lose him.

Now in all this talk of knowing a person or a place or a complex product like a book or work of art we notice a blend of *tacit recognitive power* and *patent describing ability*. Our tacit recognitive power will by some be treated merely dispositionally, as a skill, a case of knowing-how. But this could easily be to underestimate it, for it is certainly a very remarkable skill which enables us to identify any one of several thousand different faces instantly in a way which we are quite unable to put into satisfactory words.

There is a strong echo here of a sophistry which Plato toys with in the *Euthydemus* and answers in the *Meno*.[2] The puzzle was, how can you search for the answer to a question unless you are going to be able to recognize it as the answer when you meet it? But in that case you already know the answer, and it would seem therefore to be impossible to acquire any fresh knowledge. Socrates does not deny that we have a great stock of tacit knowledge, and he formulates his doctrine of *anamnesis*. Indeed we have tacit knowledge of great importance to us, but far from being a reason for indolence this is a reason for making great efforts to remind ourselves of it, to recollect it. Indeed we know more than we realize, more than we can tell, it is all there if we can but lay hold of it and bring it to the light.

[1] 1949 (Penguin ed. 1969, p. 80).
[2] I am much indebted at this stage in my argument to the recent writings of Michael Polanyi.

The puzzle Plato talks of in the *Meno* is reflected in ambiguities in the meanings of words. The "eristics" in the dialogue played with the double sense of the verb *manthanein* which can mean either to *learn* or to *understand*. If you tell me something and I understand you, I take your meaning, don't I show thereby that I already knew what you have just told me? The *wise* can be those who are apt to learn, and also those who are learned. *Learning* can be the process of learning, or that which the learned have acquired.[1] *Recognition* is often used to refer to a *first* acknowledgement of something (as in "diplomatic recognition" or the recognition of a new sub-species of a beetle) but we also use *recognition* with reference to an occasion when an acquaintance is renewed, and we "know again".

Plato's point is partly one about language: if I have a vocabulary of a few thousand words and an understanding of syntax I have the power to frame and to understand an indefinitely large number of statements. An immense field is opened to me whose boundaries seem to recede as I traverse it. All of us who have mastered a language have at our disposal a tool which we know how to use and whose power is almost unlimited. This gives us an immense potential knowledge: we have it at our disposal, latent.

Well now, what is it to know a person? I can know what someone looks like, as I can know that I shall recognize a tune when I hear it, even though I cannot fully articulate what I know. But ordinarily I cannot claim to know someone *well* unless I can say something, perhaps a good deal, about him. It seems possible to claim to know a person, a place, a picture of which I have not previously had direct experience: for it is possible, if I know enough about someone, to claim that "I know that I shall know him when I see him" and that in this sense I *do* know him.

There has been a distinction, popular among theologians, between an "I-Thou" kind of knowing, knowledge by acquaintance or direct experience, and an "I-It" kind of

[1] See A. E. Taylor's commentary in his *Plato* (1926 *et plur. all.*).

knowing, knowledge by description or knowing-that. The distinction entered theology through Martin Buber's famous book *I and Thou* (*Ich und Du*, 1923). Probably Buber has been misunderstood and misused more often than not. Certainly the distinction between encounter-knowing and propositional knowing has often been clumsily drawn. In practice our talk about knowing people reveals a complex intertwining of tacit recognizing-ability knowledge and patent describing-ability knowledge. They are woven together, and each sustains the other. Recognition comes with a shock and forces a cry or exclamation from our lips. It gives us a subject of which to predicate our descriptive phrases, enabling us to tell out what we can tell. But it is not infallible, and our descriptions act as a control upon it.

Now Christians talk of knowing God through Christ, or of knowing Christ. Such talk implies not only the ability to recognize in a face-to-face meeting but also the power to recognize effects, to interpret tell-tale signs and say to oneself "That's a bit of old so-and-so's work, I'd know it anywhere". And the primary sense of the word *recognition* does not require previous acquaintance, as a glance at the dictionary shows.

It is often supposed that a man who claims to know Christ must have had some direct experience of Christ, perhaps by supernatural means. And then the objection is raised that "I have seen Christ in a vision" behaves much more like a psychological report than like an "objective empirical judgement", in Kant's terminology. Thus claims to knowledge through visions fall down. There is no way of testing whether they are veridical. They cannot deliver enough evidence to justify the conclusion.[1]

But this is all beside the point. We have suggested that the criteria for "A knows B" might be (i) A is quite sure that he will know (be able to recognize) B without difficulty or hesitation when occasion arises; (ii) A will be able to pick out B from others, to identify him as this one and not

[1] C. B. Martin, *Religious Belief* (1959), Chap. 5.

that one; (iii) A is able to talk sense about B, to detect signs of his activity and so on.

So when Christians talk of knowing Christ I do not think they need necessarily be understood to be claiming direct acquaintance with him.

There are certainly difficulties in claiming that we will be able to recognize God when we see him. But it is not *nonsensical* to claim that a Christian knows Christ in this sense, and through Christ God, in so far as Christ is God-revealing. The claim has a clear meaning, and may be tested by the way he lives, and perhaps at last verified.

There are degrees here; for a man may know his New Testament more or less well, and he may live the relation to Christ, and apply the notions of Christ's presence and saving power with more or less of imaginative discernment and moral seriousness. If the knowledge of Christ depended upon a particular moment of acquaintance it would not be so obviously a matter of degree as it is, and it has often been made a reproach against sects which emphasize conversion that they do not pay enough attention to the need for subsequent growth. In fact, claims to know Christ do not seem necessarily to presuppose a moment of conversion to begin the acquaintance, just as we argued earlier that the claim that Jesus is risen and is now Christ does not seem necessarily to presuppose the truth of a claim that an Apostle has become acquainted with the risen Jesus in a resurrection-appearance.[1] Knowing Christ is more a matter of knowing about Jesus who is the Christ, and living out that knowledge, in the Christian community and under its guidance, in a way which involves imagination, affections and will.

At the beginning of this chapter we set ourselves two

[1] Even if a man does see Christ in a vision we still need a test of the genuineness of the vision. But the accepted tests of the genuineness of a vision, such as its moral effects, are no more than tests of the genuineness of the Christian. Being a true believer is prior to, and so may be independent of, having true visions.

questions: where is Christ, and how can people claim to know him? We deferred the first, and took the second. If we can give an intelligible account of what is meant by a claim to know Christ, that might help us to determine what sort of status should be assigned to him. We have, I hope, given an account of the meaning of talk of knowing Christ, but it has not as yet taken us very far in answering the first question.

13

ANALOGICAL KNOWLEDGE OF GOD THROUGH CHRIST

THE WORD "religion" is one of the most elastic in the language and attempts to define the essence of religion are notoriously unsuccessful. But for my present argument I need to pick out one feature of religion which I think of fundamental importance. So I shall have to justify it carefully.

What features of a work of art such as a poem or a novel might lead a critic to call it religious? Some relevant ones might be the following: a sense of evil, a sense of lost innocence (expressed perhaps through the mind of a traveller or *emigré* or in a nostalgia for childhood), a sense of desperation at the urgency and yet insolubility of moral issues, anxiety about sanity or identity, a sense of alienation (i.e. loneliness) and small unnoticed sorrows, a compassionate attitude on the part of the author towards his characters, a sense or missed opportunity, blighted hopes, greatness and littleness, incommunicable longings, the nearness of death.

It is a rather mixed and gloomy bag. Whether a particular work should be called religious or not is no doubt often largely a matter of words. Obviously these traits are more prominent in Dostoyevsky's work than in that of Henry James but in many cases the matter is more finely balanced. One could hardly imagine a novel with no trace of these characteristics.

But now we must make a distinction. Sometimes the adjective "religious" suggests the flavour of a large family of wants, yearnings and griefs. But at other times we use the word "religious" to describe an institution which sets out to assuage or relieve religious feelings. That is, the term "religious" can be used to qualify either the gap or the institution which sets out to fill it.[1]

The large family of feelings, needs, perceptions which we roughly qualify as religious are in some measure universal to men. They are especially prominent in many agnostics and atheists, almost in caricature in the prose of Russell and the verse of Housman. The longings are all the more prominent because the man is so concerned to insist upon the falsity and insufficiency of the prevailing orthodox beliefs and rites which pretend to meet them. Religious to the point of affectation in one sense, he is quite irreligious in the other.

On the other hand, Jane Austen is a religious writer in the opposite sense. That is, for her and her characters the truth and adequacy of a particular religion is so thoroughly taken for granted that many critics do not notice it. Because her work lacks the Dostoyevsky dimension it is thought irreligious. In fact it is religious, but in the sense of having a religion rather than in the sense of needing religion. But on the whole good writers who are religious in the sense of needing religion are much more common in modern times than good writers who are religious in the sense that their work is informed by a particular religion in a way which is artistically satisfactory.

Now one thing people are trying to do in religion is, in Russell's phrase, "to humanize the universe". They need to feel at home in the world, to make of the cosmos a household in which they will enjoy something like familial relations with the unknown and terrifying powers which govern human destiny. The gods need to be domesticated, or men need to become servants in the divine household: the gods need to be humanized or men to be divinized. Perhaps some kind of contract or covenant, perhaps some god-ordained ritual can do it.

At any rate, the ways in which men try to tame and

---

[1] This distinction was made by F. D. E. Schleiermacher.

come to terms with the capricious powers seem to resemble the ways in which children are socialized, that is, learn to understand and cope with adults. There have been attempts to test this hypothesis empirically. For a given society, given a number of child-training variables is it possible to predict some features of the religious institutions in that society? Some would say yes, and here is why the anthropomorphic imagery in a religion is so important and pervades its rites, beliefs, customs and teachings. It is very important that there should be terms, human terms, upon which gods and men can do business and establish a *modus vivendi*.

In religion there is, in A. S. Byatt's phrase[1], an effort to "familiarize the terrible" and the very devout can succeed in this till they attain a suffocatingly cosy domesticity. They do not realize how deeply false their humour, which expresses their confidence in their power to handle the sacred, seems to outsiders.

Attitudes to analogy are implied here. The devout have humanized God and made him manageable. The outsider thinks this an illusion: the terrible remains terrible and strange, and it is truer to experience to say so.

Religion meets various needs, and is important to a person in so far as he is conscious of them and in a religion finds them met. These needs have always been very various. There are material needs, for protection against drought, famine and plague; emotional needs, for the relief of painful feelings; cognitive needs, for a myth, a metaphysical frame and a structure of meaning; moral and social needs, for order, stability and belonging; and no doubt more too.

Some at least of these needs may be met in what we should probably want to call non-religious ways. Nationalism may give a people a sense of corporate identity and purpose. Fertilizers may displace fertility rites, and psychiatry may be more successful than lustrations in achieving a reduction of anxiety. But religious needs and religious institutions have been so various that he would be a bold man who

[1] From her recent novel, *The Game* (1967), Chapter 4.

asserted confidently that all of them will eventually find non-religious surrogates.

With the appearance of theism something new appears. Religion postulates supernatural powers who are like us. Their deeds can be recounted in myths in which they resemble human agents; they can be dealt with in human terms in prayers and rituals; and it is possible to enter into moral relations with them. They are, as it were, denizens of the same world as we, and are subject to at least some of the necessities which bind us. But theism, though to some extent it continues these old themes, also insists that God is unlike us. Typically, it regards God as creator of, and therefore independent of, the order in which we live. So from its inception monotheism made certain basic affirmations. It forbade idolatry, it was exclusive, and it insisted upon God's sovereignty, freedom, transcendence, invisibility and omnipresence. Being exalted above the world-order in which we live, God to some extent slipped out of the reach of language. What was said of him implied logical rules governing discourse about him which were such as to make that discourse perpetually incomplete and unsatisfactory. Indeed these rules verged from the beginning upon atheism, for they suggested a bar upon any claim clearly to have apprehended God or to be able to achieve any really clear expression in language of what he is. He could never be captured and domesticated.

The bar itself had odd logical features. Consider for example, what is said in the Old Testament about "seeing God". We are never very clear whether the meaning is that it is logically impossible to see God, or whether it is that it is forbidden to see God, so that you might indeed see God but would be punished for it. Similarly one is often uncertain whether idolatry is to be regarded as absurd and comical, or terribly sinful; whether the gods of other nations are real, or simply do not exist; whether the true God is jealous for his people's sake, or for his own.

Theism then is bipolar. At one pole it is practical,

anthropomorphic and continues the themes of older religions. At the other pole it prophetically transcends religion altogether. At one pole God is *near*; at the other he is *far*.

In its practical mood theism insists that God must be like us, he must make human sense if he is to be spoken of, and if his purposes and ours are to intertwine so that he can inspire the moral life, kindle the affections and imagination, and give human life a frame of meaning, a destiny. Practical theistic religion must presuppose some kinship between God and men. There must be such a moral community between God and men if God is to be represented as hating sin and loving virtue, as condemning, or forgiven and saving. If God is quite unlike us the notion of sin, as repugnant to him, is meaningless.

So in this practical mood theism is still willing to talk mythically. It will tell a great story of the dealings of God with men, a story in which both God and men are actors. The story seeks to justify the ways of God with men. From the author of the books of Samuel through Paul, Irenaeus, Athanasius, Augustine, Anselm, Dante, Calvin, Luther and Barth—even those who most stressed the transcendence of God have still thought it right to try to tell the story in a way which makes human sense. The story shows, or purports to show, that we are justified in speaking of God in human terms, even that God's policy is morally justified in human terms. Even if Milton found himself in very serious trouble few theists would say that he should not have made the attempt at all, for if no such story can be told God is nothing to us.

But in so far as the story is told successfully and convincingly it has made of God not God but a man.

And so in its transcendent or prophetic mood theism is iconoclastic, it must negate its own symbolism, it must insist upon the inexpressibility and the mysteriousness of God. It must denounce the story, it must show that theodicy is forbidden, it is presumptuous and preposterous. The authors of *Job* endorse Job's complaint, his demand that

God shall show himself, appear at and answer to a human tribunal: but the wisdom of the book is that it insists still more upon the monstrous absurdity of the demand Job makes and shows him at last repenting, repenting not his sins but his presumption in requiring God to be human. There is tragedy in the book, in a way that partly echoes but in other respects is very different from the structure of classical tragedy. The book sees tragedy in the relation of man to God in that Job must make such a demand and is right to make it—and yet must also learn in tears that the demand is absurd and wrong.

God's thoughts are not our thoughts, his ways are not our ways. The prohibition of images means that there can be no adequate concrete expression of God and no visible absolute authority in matters of faith. The image of God as in perpetual movement suggests that there can be no fixed positions and no incorrigible formulations of doctrine. All statements about God are radically defective: they cannot but be, for their subject cannot be indicated or defined clearly, and the meaning of what is asserted of him cannot be fully specified. These logical defects of all statements about God are not accidental: they are the very point of theism. For what God is is not so much expressed in our success in speaking about him as rather indirectly suggested by our failure. As Augustine said, we know him indirectly by seeing how it comes about that we do not know him.

And so in an earlier chapter we proposed as an image of God the paradoxical image of a man, perhaps in grief, breaking an image of God.

This bipolar character of theism is well illustrated in the poetry of the second Isaiah, who within a few lines can be found insisting strongly upon God's incomparability and so ineffability and yet also using the boldest anthropomorphic language.

It can also find expression in humour, as in Jesus' parables. In St. Luke there is a parable of an unjust judge who is finally driven to act by the importunity of a widow.[1] From what we know of his teaching it is highly improbable that Jesus thought of God as unjust, indolent, or slow to respond to human need: and indeed every detail of the parable is contradicted elsewhere in the tradition of Jesus' teaching. God is just, approachable, quick to act and prayer need not be nagging and repetitious. So the humour lies in the fact that it is religiously apt and fitting to command prayer to God in terms which are objectively obviously comical. Indeed you could hardly be said to have understood the parable unless you had grasped its absurdity. If you did not see the funny side of it you might have taken it to be commending the behaviour of the priests of Baal on Mount Carmel.

So the tragi-comedy of theism is that the believer must take seriously at one level what he knows at another level to be comical. In Kierkegaard's phrase, he must strive with all his might in the knowledge that his striving is but a jest. And one of the tasks of theology is the seemingly preposterous one of relating the relative, anthropomorphic deity of practical religion to the absolute, transcendent God. It has to find some kind of provisional or partial justification for the use of human terms to speak of God.

The classical answer to this question was to maintain on metaphysical grounds that the concept of being is analogical and can be extended sufficiently to embrace both God and creature. There is an analogy of being between God and man, some kind of proportionality between the way God is God and the way a creature is a creature. So it was held that there could be a corresponding logical proportionality between the way predicates might be ascribed to God and the way corresponding predicates might be ascribed to a man. The way God is good, wise or loving is apt to what God is, as the way a man may be good, wise or loving may be apt to what a man is.

Unfortunately, however this doctrine be stated it is either

[1] 18: 1–7.

vacuous or in violation of the first axiom of theism. If we say that "God is p and Socrates is p" we must be either putting God and Socrates together in the class of things that are p, or, if we say that the p-ness of God is God's sort of p-ness and the p-ness of Socrates is a human sort of p-ness, then p is being predicated quite equivocally and its meaning as predicated of God remains unknown. It is not surprising that the underlying metaphysical notion of the analogy of being should have been so offensive to many theologians. Theism postulates a radical difference between Creator and creature: God does not create out of himself, but calls into being *ex nihilo*, not out of anything at all, something quite distinct from himself. Any attempt at a philosophical justification of analogical predication is an attempt to bridge the unbridgeable gap between God and man. To put God and man together into the class of things which are and link them by an analogy of being is to break with theism. To say then that God's way of being p and a man's way of being p are quite distinct is to break again the link which has just been made. In fact, doctrines of the analogy of being, in so far as they have been subtly made, contain in themselves a dialectic of asserting and denying community between God and man. They carry, concealed within them and still unanswered, the problem they purport to solve.

So it was not only the downfall of Aristotelianism in the seventeenth century, but its own inner weakness, which has caused the theory of an analogy of being to be regarded as a failure. The commonest response to the resulting gap has been a heightened emphasis upon authority. The anthropomorphic imagery through which we relate ourselves to God is incapable of rational justification. In H. L. Mansel's terminology, it is not speculatively true: but it may nevertheless be regulatively true. The imagery may be used because it is *authorized*, it is to be believed and obeyed. Subsequently it may receive some sort of confirmation by being found to work well in practice.

We have argued against this that no satisfactory justification can be given of the claims to authority of the Bible, the church or whatever else is supposed to be the authoritative source of action-guiding religious imagery. The logical objections to the theory of an infallible authority in matters of faith were clearly grasped long ago by William Chillingworth.[1]

But in any case, what we said of the nature of theism suggested that no complete justification of our language about God should be looked for. If it could be accomplished it would overthrow theism. So theists can only seek a provisional and relative justification of religious imagery. For they insist on the hiddenness and elusiveness of God, and God does not *happen* to be hidden in such a way that he *might* be exposed. He *is* his hiddenness. A mode of speaking about God free from the inescapable logical oddities of all talk about God would not be a mode of speaking about *God*. So that paradoxically the weakness of the best accounts of the *analogia entis* is their strength. It is in a way a *merit* of St. Thomas Aquinas' account of analogy that it is so shot through with agnosticism that it repeats rather than solves the problem!

Nevertheless theism on its practical side must insist that we *are* justified in speaking of God as good, or as loving. Here enters the vehemence to which we have referred more than once, and the insistence of Barth on the humanity, the *Mitmenschlichkeit*, the with-man-ness of God. God really is good and loving, it is insisted, and yet the other pole of theism, undeterred, still retorts that we do not know and cannot explain what is meant by such talk.

In modern times theologians have laid great stress on the doctrines of revelation and of the incarnation as having at least a bearing on the problem of analogy. But very often they are formulated in such a way that it is hard to see how *God* could be the one who reveals himself, and *God* the one who is incarnate.

[1] R. R. Orr, *Reason and Authority: The Thought of William Chillingworth* (1967).

I believe Kierkegaard, in his notions of "indirect communication" and of the "incognito" of Christ, did grasp the way in which revelation and incarnation must be *indirect* or paradoxical in some sense if it is to be said without contradiction that the one who reveals, and the one who becomes incarnate, is God. But too often the notions of revelation and incarnation are presented in a way subversive of theism. The repugnance which Moslems and Jews have felt has been well-founded. For it is sometimes suggested, in talk of revelation, that by it the limits of theological discourse can be overcome; or that in it God can truly be heard speaking and assuring us in his own words that he really is human after all. Those who were a moment ago insisting that God is necessarily hidden are suddenly heard saying that in revelation God exhibits himself directly. Those who were denying the adequacy of any concrete image of God and criticizing idolatry are now heard saying that Jesus of Nazareth, or Jesus Christ, is the one certified genuine image of God. Jesus is what God is *really* like.

Our argument suggests that we should unhesitatingly dismiss such talk. What kind of revelation *can* there be of a God who is hidden and must remain so? Only the same kind as there is in the language of theism itself. What kind of act, or course of human life could be an expression in human terms of what God is? Only something puzzling and indirect, like an act of iconoclasm, or the life of a man of faith. The only possible revelation of the God of theism must be indirect.

Materially the man who believes in God struggles to express and realize in the course of his life a human moral relation to God. He lives as if God sees, God is just and loving and will in the end vindicate faith. The imagery through which he thinks and lives his relation to God is a frail boat in which he ventures out upon the sea not knowing how far it is capable of bearing him. *Formally*, or logically, the equivalent of this question is, how far can one be justified in pretending to speak of *God* in human terms?

Early Christianity replied to this question by putting forward its most original and striking creation, the literary form of a Gospel: a theological narrative of the life and death of Jesus.

At least, then, the Gospel is a story. How can a story be informative? What is the relation between the story and the beliefs about God which it is held to validate?

The fact that the historian is a story-teller who explains the past by making a story of it has been emphasized in some recent writings on the philosophy of history.[1] And the way in which a group of people are held together by sharing a myth which explains who they are, and why they belong together is generally recognized. The function of the Gospel-story in Christianity is plainly related to these things. But an inkling of how it works can be gained from a much older source.

In his Poetics Aristotle writes about the theory of tragedy.[2] In the finest tragedies, which he perhaps rather awkwardly calls "complex" tragedies, it is the plot that counts; and the distinctive feature of a good plot is the presence in it of what he calls a *peripeteia* and/or an *anagnōrisis*. A *peripeteia*, sometimes called a "reversal", occurs when the protagonist suffers a reversal of fortune or finds himself plunged into a situation in which he struggles and suffers not knowing the outcome. *Anagnōrisis* or "recognition" occurs when the true meaning of what has been happening is made plain, often by the disclosure of the true identity of one of the characters. The play proceeds from ignorance through suffering to knowledge.

Sometimes the audience knows or is able to guess the truth before the characters do, and hence arises *irony*. In the finest tragedies the whole plot is organized in terms of these two concepts, of reversal and recognition.

---

[1] A. C. Danto, *Analytical Philosophy of History* (1965); and W. B. Gallie, *Philosophy and the Historical Understanding* (1964).

[2] See the very full edition, with text, commentary, etc., by D. W. Lucas (1968).

The recognition may be brought about in various ways, and one notices that the New Testament narratives of the resurrection exemplify all of them. There are five sorts of recognition, and though Aristotle's text is brief and far from perfect they seem to be as follows:

The *first* is the production of a mark or token, such as a birthmark or scar;

The *second* is a personal confession of identity, contrived by the poet;

The *third* is "through memory" when the unknown man betrays his identity by a characteristic gesture, or when he sees something which reminds him of the past and betrays himself by showing his feelings;

The *fourth* is by inference, as when only one conclusion can be drawn from the discovery of a certain object in a certain place;

And the *fifth* case is that where "the structure of the plot is such that as it develops the true identity is necessarily revealed".[1]

As for examples, it is by a scar that Odysseus' identity is made known to his old nurse, and Jesus' to Thomas: Orestes tells Iphigenia who he is, and so Jesus declares his own identity: Odysseus weeps on hearing the song about the Wooden Horse, and Jesus betrays himself by the way he says "Mary", or breaks bread: Electra makes an inference from a lock of hair on her father's tomb, and the beloved disciple from what he sees in Jesus' tomb.

Aristotle's classification is clumsy and over-rigid, but he thinks the last sort of recognition the best. And the kind of inevitability he speaks of is prominent in the gospels. There is a good example of it in the story of the walk to Emmaus. Given scriptural foreshadowings, given the actual course of Jesus' life to its end, given all that has happened, how can Jesus *not* be risen and Christ? But the obviousness of it was not at all apparent to the disciples, "foolish men and slow of heart" as they were. And so the stranger on the road

[1] Lucas, p. 172.

laboriously goes over the ground, paints the picture, sets this beside that, points out the obvious, until the climax is reached in the quasi-Eucharistic conclusion of the story when all the elements in the jigsaw fall into place. It is natural that Rembrandt, in his drawing in the Fitzwilliam Museum in Cambridge, should represent this moment as a flash of light like an explosion. The flash does not stand on its own: it is absurd to base belief in the resurrection on the resurrection-appearances. To understand the epistemology of the flash you have to go over the whole argument again. Only when the whole argument is grasped, seen in the right way, is the necessity of it understood: the Son of Man *must* suffer, Jesus *must* be the Christ, the Lord *must* be risen.[1] And the necessity here is a kind of dramatic necessity which can be grasped by those who have ears to hear, those who see in the compelling force of the story the meaning of their own lives.

The way in which the gospel, that Jesus is the living Christ, is hidden in the Gospels is like the way in which the meaning of a parable is hidden in the parable. It is something like the relation of evidence to conclusion, word to meaning, thing looked at to thing seen. You are looking at something, but what do you *see*? You are listening to something, but what do you *hear*? You are presented with a body of material, but what do you *make* of it?

Take the case of a parable. Nathan told David a story about a rich man who stole a poor man's only ewe lamb. He told the story not so much to *make* a statement as to *elicit* a statement. If David had said, "I am the man," instead of having to be told, "Thou art the man," he would have "heard" the parable in the sense required in the Gospels. In that case the parable would have told him something, indirectly. It was a device which seized his imagination and led him to a standpoint from which he could see clearly something which in a way he knew already.

[1] St Luke makes this point about the logic of the resurrection faith again in 24: 44–8.

I'm not sure that we would call this news, or information. Rather, the parable cunningly removed his resistance to acknowledging something which he knew perfectly well, but did not want to know.

Did the Gospel parables convey information? Yes, in a way they told the good news that God is near, he comes to judge and save, he is merciful and so on. But they told it indirectly. Being told, the parable hangs in the air, like a question, inviting the listener to make something of it. Whether we say that the man who "hears" the parable has gained fresh information, or that he has learnt to see old things in a new light does not matter very much—provided that the full importance of what has happened to him is understood. He is a changed man because he now sees God in a new way, thinks of God in new ways, begins to live differently.

Then what of the gospel-story as a whole, the story of Jesus: how might *that* change the way people think of God? How do they come to see in it not merely a mythological, but an historically enacted, paradigm of the relation of men to God which even *changes* that relation for us all?

Perhaps somewhat as follows: commitment to the life of faith is commitment to the belief that God is *near*—that a moral relation to him can be lived out in human life. To do such a thing in Jesus' day was to swim against the stream. Belief in God and his goodness—that is, his *nearness* —had been from time immemorial axiomatic, but for centuries it had been under severe strain. The bitter daily experience of national decline and disaster, the unrequited suffering of the humble who still hoped doggedly for divine deliverance, had led Jewish thought into increasing preoccupation with the problem of evil. God seemed withdrawn, distant and hostile. His proper name was no longer spoken.

Under the trial of faith religion developed in various ways. The cult might become formal and ritualized. Scepticism might develop. Among the devout who felt bitterly the contradiction between fact and faith people might draw strength and the will to live from imagining an imminent catastrophe. They lived on credit, for there was no sustenance in the present. God was far and if he ever came near it would be to overthrow, to burn up and to annihilate. Messianic claimants arose and fell in their own blood. Ascetical sects artificially heightened the torment in order to hasten the end by forcing God to act. The world was seen as under the dominion of evil powers. A veiled suspicion of God, mistrust of him, ran beneath the expectation of his coming to destroy the world.

In this strange context Jesus' message of the nearness of God was not just another variation on the apocalytic theme. The apocalyptist wrote pseudonymously; Jesus spoke in his own person. The apocalyptist pictured God as an implacable majesty, an irresistible force; Jesus' preaching was extremely anthropomorphic. God's reign was near, he was righteous, merciful, loving, and he made an urgent claim upon each individual. The existing religious system had an interest in representing God as far; but for Jesus God was near. So in Jesus' preaching there was a thoroughgoing attempt to affirm the nearness and goodness of God in an age which could not but believe the opposite.

The preaching aroused opposition: it raised up the demons of hostility and mistrust. The people of God could not bear the nearness of God. And Jesus' own living out of his anthropomorphic faith disclosed that its own logic led to its own loss. In obedience to God as he conceived God, Jesus was obliged to lose the imagery, to experience the distance of God, the Messianic Woes and the Cross. The optimistic imagery which pictured God as fatherly, good and loving, if it was lived, led to its own renunciation. In the oldest form of the Passion Narrative, the nucleus of the gospels, God's continuing command of events is stressed, but that command is actually felt as an enigmatic and harsh necessity. In St. Mark Jesus does not understand what is happening to him, and is not in command of events: his plight is truly tragic. The Messiah *must* suffer before he can enter his kingdom and true suffering is incomprehensible to the sufferer. The man who spoke of God with such intimacy and authority finds he is irresistibly led to experience the extreme opposite condition. Only through undergoing such a test can such a faith be decisively vindicated.

If we ask the question, what kind of justification of our analogical discourse about God can there be, the Gospels return a curious answer. They represent Jesus as living out the relation to God through a certain set of anthropomorphic images—and the logic of the images was such that, followed through, they led to their own loss. They were self-transcending. If they are justified it is because they do point beyond themselves, to Calvary and Easter.

If Christian theology is to explain what Jesus Christ is for Christians it must begin from this point, that he supremely exhibits what it is to have to do with God, and he shows what kind of testing our analogical discourse about God must undergo before it can be validated. Christians believe that Jesus is the Christ, and still lives now, and still actively relates men to God because they discern in the narratives of his life and death the epitome of the universal human situation before God, the Yes and the No, the nearness and the farness. To tease this out in detail is the task of theologians, and the history of Christian thought, with all its blind alleys, false starts, eccentricities and follies, is an attempt to do it.

In conclusion, what is the present reference of talk of Christ? Our argument has led us to this position. Christ now is not indicable, nor can his existence be inferred in a valid argument. Talk of the present Christ could have a reference and does have a use, but that reference cannot be satisfactorily established. The believer gives it an historical reference: Christ is none other than Jesus, exalted as Lord. And he gives it a present use. For the rest, he believes that he knows Christ in the sense that he will recognize him when he sees him, and that he now knows God through him.

INDEX